George Saintsbury

Primer of French Literature

Third Edition

George Saintsbury

Primer of French Literature
Third Edition

ISBN/EAN: 9783337205355

Printed in Europe, USA, Canada, Australia, Japan

Cover: Foto ©Thomas Meinert / pixelio.de

More available books at **www.hansebooks.com**

Clarendon Press Series

PRIMER

OF

FRENCH LITERATURE

BY

GEORGE SAINTSBURY

THIRD EDITION, REVISED

Oxford

AT THE CLARENDON PRESS

1888

PREFACE TO THE SECOND EDITION.

THE first edition of this little book appeared without a preface: the second may perhaps be allowed one, if only to express the Author's thanks to his critics and to the public for the reception given to his work. Some corrections of phrase have been made, and a few errors in the dates have been rectified. That such corrections have not been more numerous is, I believe, mainly owing to the great care with which my friend Mr. Andrew Lang read the proof sheets for me and to the valuable suggestions which he made. In deference to the request of several friends an index has been added, though I myself consider the addition somewhat superfluous in the case of a book the body of which is little more than an index in itself. I have limited it to those names in connection with which something more than a mere mention will be found in the text. For the compiling of this index I owe my best thanks to Miss Emily J. Carey; while for indicating to me a somewhat important omission in a passage relating to Pascal I am obliged to M. Paul Stapfer, Professor in the Faculty of Letters at Grenoble.

PREFACE TO THE THIRD EDITION.

IN this third edition the text has been again carefully revised, and some corrections made. It has not however been thought well to encumber a book intended for beginners with too many details and provisos referring to the now rapidly accumulating, but not always certain or unanimous, opinions of Old-French scholars on points respecting the date and authorship of mediaeval work. As the greater part of a decade has passed since the book was first written, a few passages, dealing with writers who have made their mark in the interval, have been inserted in the later pages, and several death-dates have been added.

GEORGE SAINTSBURY.

CONTENTS.

CHAPTER I.

(FRENCH literature has at the present day a history which extends over a little more than eight centuries.) A few isolated documents can be produced which throw this history back somewhat further. But from the eleventh century onwards there is no break in the story, and the literature of France occupies a position which is almost unique. Other countries, for instance our own, can boast of a literary pedigree nominally longer. But there is one great difference which separates French from English literary history. No Englishman to-day can appreciate the earliest English literature, or any English literature before the fourteenth century, without a special training quite as laborious as has to be gone through in the case of a foreign language. Any Frenchman, or any one who has acquired a fair knowledge of modern French, can, with no special instruction and with only a very little trouble, read the very earliest French literary monuments. (The *Chanson de Roland*, which is at least as old as the Norman Conquest, can be read with not more difficulty by the one, than Chaucer, who is four hundred years later in date, by the other.) Another peculiarity of early French literature is its extraordinary richness and variety. With little foreign influence or admixture, the French in the middle ages produced specimens of almost

B

every kind of literary work that we now have, and some of
these rank among the best of their kind. Hence the study
of French literature is among the most interesting of all
literary studies, because we see in it what a nation can
achieve with the minimum of foreign aid.

The reason why French literature does not date so early
as English is that the language in which it is written is not
an original tongue, but a corruption of Latin. The conquest
of Gaul by the Romans, unlike the conquest of Britain, was
so thorough that, except in remote corners of the land, the
old tongue spoken by the Gauls was quite driven out. The
new tongue brought in by the conquerors was gradually
changed until what we call French arose out of Latin. It
seems probable that something like a new language came of
this change by the seventh century, but the first certain
instance of it that we have is much later. A language, called
Lingua Romana or Romance tongue, to distinguish it from
Lingua Latina or Latin, was sufficiently established in 842 for
it to be necessary for the two sons of Charlemagne's son,
when they made a treaty together at Strasburg, to have a
copy of the agreement made in French. The language of
the 'Strasburg Oaths,' as they are called, is very strange to
those who know French only or Latin only, but to those
who know both it is easy enough. Soon afterwards the new
language became sufficiently popular for poems to be written
in it. There is a hymn or poem of great beauty on the
martyrdom of St. Eulalia which dates from the tenth century
at least, and possibly from the ninth. It tells how Eulalia, the
maiden *bel avret corps, bellezour anima*—had a fair body and
a fairer soul; how the enemies of God strove to pervert her,
but for no threat or promise would she listen to them. *Por
manatce regiel ne preimen*—for royal menace nor prayer would
she become a heathen. So she was brought before Maximian

the Emperor and sentenced to the flames. But the fire would not touch her, and they had to behead her with a sword. And then in the shape of a dove her soul fled to the skies, *in figure de colomb volat ad ciel*. This is the earliest or almost the earliest piece of really literary work that can be called French, and we have a few other pieces of the same period, mostly religious in kind. There is a poem on the Passion, one on the life of St. Leger, and, in the form of French which we now call Provençal, a poem on the philosopher Boethius. All these date from the tenth century, and before that there is nothing certain except the oaths already mentioned and a few lists of words, dictionaries as it were, to tell foreigners what were the equivalents in the new Romance tongue of the words familiar to them either in Latin or in German.

But when France was once for all separated from Germany, and when the Normans had settled themselves in the north, and the Spanish Arabs had been thoroughly beaten back behind the Pyrenees, it was natural that the French should set to work to make a literature of their own. The very first kind of literature that they tried to write was of great and remarkable interest. No nation in the world has anything that can compare with what are called the *Chansons de Gestes*. These Chansons de Gestes—songs of families, as the term literally means[1]—are poems, most of them of great length, describing the history and achievements of the great men of France in early times. Most of them have to do with the deeds of Charlemagne or of his son, but some are concerned with the fierce battles of the feudal lords who from a very early time divided France between them, and the

---

[1] *Geste* has three senses—(1) the deeds (*gesta*) of a hero; (2) the poem illustrating those deeds; (3) the family of the hero and the set of poems celebrating it.

latest deal with the first Crusade, in which Frenchmen bore
so large a share.   These Chansons de Gestes are not mere
rude stories or legends.   They are written in regular verse,
nearly as polished and careful as that which Englishmen and
Frenchmen write now.   But there is one curious thing about
them. ⌊The older ones are not rhymed, but are written in
what is called *assonance.*⌋ This means that though the last
syllables of the lines have the same vowel-sound there is
not the same arrangement of consonants in them.   Sometimes nowadays, when writers who do not know what they
are about try to write English poetry, they make such rhymes
as 'war' and 'law,' 'time' and 'thine.'   These are very bad
rhymes, but they would be very good assonances.   Sometimes indeed in reading a Chanson de Geste one has to think
a little even to see the assonance, because all the vowels were
not pronounced then quite in the same way as they are now.
But this does not at all interfere with the beauty of these
poems.   They are often of very great length, and the oldest
and best of them all, the *Chanson de Roland*, which tells how
Roland and Oliver and many more of Charlemagne's paladins
died at Roncesvaux through the treachery of Ganelon, is
about four thousand lines long.   Some of the others are
much longer.   For it was a curious habit of the French in
the middle ages, that when a poem was written which they
liked, instead of letting it alone they were always altering it
and making it longer and suiting it to the taste of the time.
So that at last the *Chansons de Gestes* got very long indeed
and not a little tiresome, some of them even extending to fifty
thousand lines, or about four times the length of *Paradise Lost.*
But the earlier ones were not so long as this, and they are
full of interest.   In *Roland* there is a splendid passage just
before the account of the hero's death.   The fight is going
on, though in France men know nothing of it.   'But none
the less in France was there great disturbance.   There was

thunder and wind, hail and rain falling heavily, and always the earth shook and trembled from St. Michael's at Paris [1] to Sens, and from Wisant to Besançon. The walls of the houses shook and there was darkness at midday, so that all men who saw it trembled and said, " the end of the world is at hand." But they were wrong, and knew not what they said, for it was the great mourning of the land for the death of Roland.' In all the older chansons the principal subject is the noble struggle unto death of Christian heroes against the Saracens. But there are many other subjects. The chief fault of the feudal system was the perpetual jealousy and disunion which it spread among the great men of the state. All these chansons bear witness to this, and show us sometimes the nobles quarrelling among themselves; sometimes the emperor prejudiced by traitors against his faithful servants. At first ladies play but a small part in these chansons, though afterwards it is different. We have in all nearly a hundred of these interesting poems, many of which are much later in date than the eleventh or even the twelfth century, but in these cases they have generally been copied and extended from others of an earlier time.

Not quite so early as these poems, but soon afterwards, there began to be written another kind of romance [2]. Among the Celtic peoples of Wales and of Brittany there had long been traditions of a great king, Arthur by name, who was supposed in the fifth century to have opposed the invasions

---

[1] This is the reading of the oldest MS., but it is doubtless a mistake for St. Michel *du Péril* (in periculo maris), i. e. Mont St. Michel in Normandy. There is also some doubt whether Sens is a proper name, or is not rather ' seins,' the old form of ' saints,' i. e. the three kings or saints of Cologne, to which latter place the phrase would then apply.

[2] It should be observed that this word indicates the character and popularity of early French literature. *Enromancer* properly means ' to turn into French.'

of the German and Scandinavian immigrants. It is possible
that some of these legends may have been written down in
the vulgar tongues, though there is no evidence to show that
any were so written earlier than the twelfth century. A
writer called Nennius had however written in bad Latin an
account of the Saxon and Anglian and Jutish invasion of
Britain, and this, with perhaps some assistance from the
legends alluded to, Geoffrey of Monmouth worked up into
his *Historia Britonum* in 1140 (?). This book became immensely popular both in France and England, and a Jersey-
man named Wace translated it into French verse under
the title of *Brut*. Soon after, the story thus given was taken
hold of by a knot of clever writers at the English and French
courts, the chief of the former being Walter Map, and the
chief of the latter Robert de Borron. These writers, many
of whom are now unknown, in the course of a few years
produced a wonderful fabric of romance on the subject of
Arthur, his Knights, and the mysterious vessel of the Saint
Graal, which was supposed to be the vessel in which Christ
had celebrated the Holy Supper, and to have been brought
into England by Joseph of Arimathea. These stories were
written in the first place, not as all stories, whether true or
false, had apparently hitherto been written, in verse, but in
prose, and in very good prose too. Still, however, most of
those who cared for stories preferred verse, and the prose
romances were soon versified. The chief of the versifiers was
Chrétien de Troyes, who lived about 1180. Chrétien was
a very busy writer, and we have a large number of his works,
besides which we know that he wrote others which are lost.
Those we have concerning Arthur are *Percevale*, a long
legend of the Holy Graal, which was continued by others till
it extended to over fifty thousand verses; *Erec et Énide*, the
pretty story which Lord Tennyson has revived in the *Idylls*

of the King ; Le Chevalier à la Charette, versified from part
of Walter Map's great book of *Lancelot du Lac,* in which
Map and perhaps some other writers told the story of the
greatest of Arthur's knights ; *Le Chevalier au Lyon,* a story of
Evan of Wales, another knight of Arthur's court ; and lastly,
Cligés, a romance, in which the son of the Emperor of Constantinople is brought to join the Table Round. These
romances, both prose and verse, are very different from the
Chansons de Gestes. In the first place, instead of being
written in assonanced verses of ten or twelve syllables, they
are written in pairs of verses of eight syllables each, rhyming
just in the same way as modern poetry does. The characters and scenery described are also very different. The
knights are much more of the kind which we now call
chivalrous than the paladins of Charlemagne. These latter
seem to care for nothing but fighting and killing infidels ;
they are rude and brutal to one another and to their wives
and lady-loves. The Arthurian knights are much more
gentle and courteous ; they delight more in single combats
and tournaments than in confused battles with the Saracens
and each other ; they are full of politeness to ladies and of
reverence for the King. There is also much more religion
in the Romances than in the Chansons, though perhaps what
there is in the latter is more sincere. The whole story of
the Holy Graal was originally a religious one, though the
spirit of chivalry has somewhat altered it. Lastly, we can see
that by the time the Arthurian Romances were written,
civilisation had advanced a good deal. Living was more
luxurious, and the classes of society were more numerous.
In the Chansons we hardly hear of any one but nobles and
peasants ; shopkeepers and citizens make their appearance
in the Romances for the first time.

Nor were Charlemagne and Arthur the only persons

whose doings occupied writers at this date. It used to be thought, and is still thought by some people, that the middle ages were ignorant of the classics and classical times. This is quite a mistake; Chrétien de Troyes wrote some translations of Ovid, and by the twelfth century there began to grow up, just as the other two kinds of romances had grown up, a whole class of poems about classical subjects. The most important by far of these is the romance of *Alixandre*, the twelve-syllabled verse of which was thought so excellent that such lines have ever since been called Alexandrines. This is a very long poem written at the end of the century by two authors, a certain Lambert and Alexander of Bernay, and it contains a very curious mixture of facts taken out of history and of fancies prevalent at the time about fairies and giants and the fountain of youth, and such like things. Another very long and very important poem is the romance of Troy by Benedict de Sainte-More, a poem written like the Arthurian romances in eight-syllabled couplets. It is of great interest to us, because it contains the original of the story of Troilus and Cressida, which two of our greatest poets, Chaucer and Shakespeare, have dealt with since. (In fact one of the most surprising things about early French poetry is the number of stories which appear in it for the first time, and which other nations have borrowed since.) Much indeed of the invention was due to Englishmen, who happened to speak and write French as the court language of the time in England; but still the books themselves belong to French literature, not to English, and were soon copied and translated by the poets of England, Italy, Germany, and all the nations of Europe besides.

It must not be supposed that the people of France as a rule read these poems. They were generally recited by a class of men and women called Jongleurs and Jongleresses, who went about from house to house repeating poetry. When these jongleurs began to play and to recite, they used to beg the audience to be silent, and to boast of the superiority of the poems they could tell to those of other jongleurs; and when they had done they would ask pretty plainly for money. Many of the manuscripts in which we have received the works of these times, are the very same which these jongleurs carried about with them, and so these curious additions have come down with the text. Those who wrote the poems were not called jongleurs, but trouveurs, though sometimes a trouveur would sing and recite his own works. By degrees rich men cared to have these poems copied for them. For this purpose they employed copyists, who wrote on great books of parchment or paper all sorts of poems, one after another, without any reference to their contents or connexion. Such manuscripts as these were too large to be carried about by jongleurs, but they have preserved to us the majority of the poems which we have. To give some idea of the immense quantity of poetry which was written at this time, it may be mentioned that what we have, though doubtless much is lost, amounts to several million lines. There is, for the time of which we are speaking, much less prose. The long Arthurian romances are almost the only long prose compositions before the thirteenth century. History was still written in Latin. But Maurice de Sully, who died in 1196, has left us sermons written in French, and there are a few translations and paraphrases of the Bible in the vernacular. One of the oldest prose works we have is a commentary on the prophet Jonah, in which French sentences are mixed up with the Latin, according to a curious but not infrequent habit of the time. There is also a translation of the Book of Kings, which dates from the twelfth century. These works were for the most part written by monks, and some of the

French monasteries became famous for the pains which were taken in them to write chronicles of present and past French history, though until about 1200 they were not written in the French language.

As men were as yet unaccustomed to write in prose, they wrote in verse a good many things which, as it seems to us now, might have been done much better in prose. Quite early in the twelfth century they began to translate and paraphrase various historical books in French verse. We have spoken of Wace's *Brut.* The same poet wrote also a very long poem called the *Roman de Rou* (Rollo), giving a history of the Dukes of Normandy and of their conquest of England. Even before Wace, another writer, Geoffrey Gaymar, had written a chronicle in verse, and after him Benedict de Sainte-More, who has also been mentioned, wrote a still longer chronicle of Normandy in eight-syllabled verses. Besides these long poems, a great many shorter ones, describing different events of the time, were composed. Thus a sketch of the conquest of Ireland was written in 1172. Nor was history the only serious subject which was thus treated. About 1125 Philippe de Thaun wrote for Queen Adela of England two curious little books, in French verse of six syllables. One used to be called *Liber de Creaturis* (now we are told to call it *Comput*), and contained an account of the calendar, and the arrangements which Cæsar and others had introduced to improve it. The other was entitled *Bestiarius*, or Beast-book. In the middle ages the knowledge of distant countries was not very full or accurate, and many strange stories, some of them beautiful enough, but few of them having much foundation of fact, were told about all real animals and a good many fabulous ones, such as unicorns and dragons. Philippe tells these stories in his brisk little verses, and to each he adds a kind of moral, treating the story as an allegory of some fact or doctrine in the Christian religion. People in the middle ages were exceedingly fond of these allegorical moralisings, and we shall hear a good deal more of them.

Besides the long romances and poems on serious subjects, of various kinds, the trouvères[1] composed many short songs and tales, some of a serious and some of a comic kind. The songs are generally divided by modern scholars under two heads, *romances* and *pastourelles*. The romance may perhaps be best described (as a song with a story in it.) It generally tells how some fair lady was won by a gallant knight in tourney or in war, and has usually at the end of each stanza what is called a refrain or burden; that is to say, the same phrase repeated without alteration. Sometimes these refrains have no particular sense, like our 'hey no nonny,' 'derry down,' etc. ; sometimes they have a meaning which connects itself with the general sense of the song. The best of these romances are attributed to an otherwise unknown writer called Audefroi le Bastard. The pastour-elles were a very favourite kind of poem, and we have great numbers of them. They generally describe how the poet, or somebody else, was riding through a beautiful country in a fine spring or summer morning, and how he saw by the roadside a fair shepherdess keeping her flocks. Then he gets down from his horse and begins to make love to her, and sometimes she accepts his love, and sometimes she says that she has already a sweetheart, some simple shepherd whom she will not desert for a stranger. Besides these there was another kind of poem, which was rather a tale than a song, and which began to be written about this

---

[1] This word (= *trouveur*) is used to distinguish the poets of Northern France from those of Southern. The term distinguishing the latter (*troubadour*) is a third form of the same.

time. This is what is called the *fabliau*. A fabliau has been
described as 'a story of some actual or possible event occur-
ring in every-day life,' and poems of this kind became great
favourites in France. Most of them were of the comic kind,
very much resembling the lighter of Chaucer's *Canterbury
Tales*, which indeed are in many cases taken from fabliaux.
Sometimes they have a moral, but not very often. The story
of Molière's *Médecin malgré lui* is found in one of the fabliaux,
and is a very good example of the kind. It tells how a
woodcutter quarrelled with his wife and beat her. So she in
revenge told some of the king's servants that her husband
was a great doctor, and he was carried off to the court, and
ordered to cure the king's daughter; out of which scrape he
got himself by his cleverness. We have an immense number
of these little poems, almost all of which are more or less
amusing, and many of which have become famous in the
more modern shape which later authors in English, Italian
and French have given them.

Still more important, perhaps, if we look at what it led to,
though much less interesting in itself, is the beginning of
play-writing, which also belongs to the twelfth century. (The
first French dramas, which are earlier than any written in
òther modern European languages, were acted in church, and
almost formed part of religious services;) consequently they
were all on sacred subjects. They had been written in
Latin, which was then the language of the church service, at
first; but as they were intended to amuse and attract the
common people, it was clearly necessary that they should
soon be written in French. For a time however Latin and
French were mixed in them as in the commentary on Jonah
which we have noticed. These dramas are called *mysteries*,
and one of the earliest, if not the earliest of all, is the mystery
of the *Ten Virgins*, in which some of the speeches are in

French. Then we have a mystery or drama of the story of *Daniel*; and at last, but still before the end of the twelfth century, there is the mystery of *Adam*, which is all written in French, though the directions to the actors are in Latin.

Thus we see that early French literature was extraordinarily abundant in amount and various in form. Although its prose is a little backward, there is hardly any kind of poetry which the trouvères had not tried, and in which they had not succeeded. To this day there are no more beautiful or more beautifully told stories than the Arthurian legends. The Carlovingian epics, as the Chansons de Gestes are sometimes called, are more monotonous and less attractive in incident and manner, but full of fierce love of battle and of the spirit of resolute independence. The songs are charmingly musical, and the fabliaux, or short comic tales, are full of fun and cleverness. The bad side of French literature however had thus early begun to show itself as well as the good. In all the popular poems, and especially in the fabliaux, women are spoken of with constant disrespect, and the baser side of their character is brought prominently forward. Except in the Arthurian stories, where Welsh and English influence is strong, there is but little imagination shown, little sense of the mysterious and the beautiful in nature, little reverence for things that are great and good. These drawbacks are compensated to some extent by the excellence of literary form and expression, which contrasts very strongly with the rough and inelegant metres and phrases of most other European languages at the time. Most striking of all perhaps is the inexhaustible invention of the French trouvères. They were never tired of devising new stories or new versions of the old ones, and it is a literal truth that for some centuries almost every country in Europe contented itself in the way of fictitious literature with translations and adaptations from the French. So popular were the Carlovingian epics, that there are several manuscripts of them written in what we may call a kind of pigeon-French, on the same principle as the pigeon-English which the Chinese talk. These manuscripts have French words with Italian terminations, and were evidently written to please the people of northern Italy.

CHAPTER II.

THE thirteenth century is considered, and rightly, to be the most flourishing period of old French literature. We cannot, of course, expect that such a period should exactly coincide with chronological divisions of an arbitrary kind. But if we borrow a few years from the end of the twelfth century and a few years from the beginning of the fourteenth, making perhaps a hundred and twenty in continuous stretch, we shall find singular excellence in almost all kinds of literature shown during this time. It may have been noticed that hitherto the greater part of French literature has been anonymous, except in the case of the Arthurian romances. We do not know who wrote the *Chanson de Roland*, or most of the older chansons; the majority of the other poems of the time are in the same way by unknown authors, and even where we have a name it is for the most part a name only, little or nothing being known of the person designated. It is very different in the time to which we are now coming, and the works of Thibaut of Champagne, Rutebœuf, Villehardouin, Joinville, and others, are made all the more interesting by the knowledge, more or less accurate, which we possess of the lives these writers led and the circumstances under which they wrote.

The Chansons de Gestes still continued to be written at this time, but they underwent a considerable change. The

language in which they had been originally composed had
become partially unintelligible, and was thought rough and
inelegant, as were the manners and customs depicted. So
the poets of the day set to work to rewrite the old chansons
as well as to write fresh ones, which were rhymed and not
merely assonanced like the old epics. A good instance
of such writers is Adenés le Roi, a trouvère of French
Flanders, who lived about 1260. Adenés is a diminutive of
Adam, and the poet has been supposed to have been called Le
Roi from his position as 'King of the Minstrels' in the Count
of Flanders' household. Adenés took three old chansons,
called *Berte aux Grands Pieds*, *La chevalerie Ogier*, and
Le Siége de Barbastre, and rewrote them under the same
title in the first place, and under those of *Les Enfances
Ogier* and *Beuves de Comarchis* in the second and third. As
it happens, we have part of the originals of *Ogier* and
Beuves de Comarchis, and therefore we are able to compare
the two ways of treatment. (The newer poems are much
smoother and more pleasantly written, the older have more
vigour and character.) The Arthurian romances also continued to be very much read, and to be lengthened and
rewritten. But the special form of long poem which the
century preferred was what is called the *Roman d'Aventures*.
In these poems, neither Charlemagne nor Arthur, nor any
hero of ancient history, forms the centre. They are almost
independent, though some attempt has been made to bring
them under two classes, one joining on to the Arthurian
story, another having to do with legends fetched from the
East during the Crusades. One of the earliest writers of
such poems was Raoul de Houdenc, whose date is not
known, but who must have lived at the extreme end of
the twelfth century. Raoul wrote, it is thought, two long
poems of adventure entitled *Méraugis de Portlesguez* and *La*

Vengeance de Raguidel, both of which are courtly Round-Table stories, and besides these some curious smaller poems of an allegorical kind. Adenés le Roi, who has just been mentioned, wrote a very long and popular romance entitled *Cléomadès.* This brings in the wooden horse flying upwards or downwards by means of pegs, which every one knows in the *Arabian Nights. Partenopex de Blois* (written, it used to be said, by Denis Pyramus, but this is now denied) is a beautiful story where the hero, like Psyche in the Greek story, loses his love for a time through foolish curiosity; while another, *Amadas et Idoine,* has for its central incident something like the fight of Death and Hercules at the tomb of Alcestis. All these poems of adventure, which are very numerous, are composed in eight-syllabled verse, generally very well written; and as there is less monotony in them than in the Chansons de Gestes it is easy to understand why they became popular, though they are much less interesting as showing us the manners of the time and have no passages quite equal to the best of the chansons. They are so numerous that it is impossible to mention all or even most of them, and many are still unprinted.

The influence of Eastern literature was felt in a good many ways about this time, especially in the shape of moral stories. There was one famous book, which came from India originally, it is thought, and being translated into Greek, was called *Syntipas.* It contained a large number of stories, supposed to be told by seven wise men to an Emperor of Rome, to persuade him not to put his son (who had been falsely accused of a crime) to death. This book got itself paraphrased into French in two ways early in the thirteenth century. The first form was in verse, and is called *Dolopathos,* from the name of the hero. This was written by a monk named Herbert, from a Latin translation made by another

C

monk, John of Hauteseille. The second form was called
The Seven Wise Men of Rome, and was originally in prose.
It supplied a good many stories for a still more famous book,
the *Gesta Romanorum*; but this, though there were versions
of it in French, is supposed to have been originally written
by an Englishman, probably in Latin. (Prose stories become
common at this time.) We have one very beautiful one called
Aucassin et Nicolette, which describes how the son of the Count
of Beaucaire fell in love with a beautiful Saracen girl, and
how, despite the opposition of his friends, they were at last
made happy. Another tells the story which Mr. Morris has
told in English verse, under the title of 'The man who was
born to be king,' and another that of Troilus and Cressida.
Most of these short stories show traces of Classical or
Eastern origin, or are prose versions of the old verse
romances.

The East also had an influence, by means not merely of
the Bible but of other sources, on the moral literature of the
time, which was considerable. At an uncertain date a book
was translated or adapted from the Arabic under the title of
Le Castoiement d'un Père—the advice of a father—embodying
various moral precepts which are enforced by stories and
examples. The pattern of the Bestiaries was still further followed up, and treatises on all kinds of arts and science began
to be written, for the most part in verse, but later also in prose.

The fancy for story-telling, and the fancy for moral
instruction and allegory, found one particular outlet in the
fable or beast-story. The fables of Esop early became
popular, and the title *Ysopet* was for a long time used for
collections of this kind. The best, and one of the first, of the
writers of such work was Marie de France. We know very
little about Marie except that she lived for the most part
at the English court, and called herself 'de France' to mark

her nationality. Her fables are very brightly and pleasantly written, but her poetical reputation does not rest solely upon them. The best work she did was her *Lais*, as they are called. The Lai was a kind of narrative poem, not very long, and 'supposed to be of Breton origin, and to have been sung to the accompaniment of a peculiar kind of music. In verse and style, as Marie wrote it, it is not distinguishable from a short romance. Most of the stories of her lays (*Lanval, Les Deux Amants, Le Chaitivel,* &c.) are very affecting, while some of them, such as *Bisclaveret*, deal with wild Breton fancies—in this case the notion of were-wolves—which lend themselves excellently to poetical treatment. There are other lays of the same kind as Marie's, and later French poets adapted the term for an altogether different and much inferior sort of poem.

While Marie was thus writing poems which were half narrative and half lyrical, lyric poetry proper was being abundantly cultivated. Quite at the beginning of the century there were two groups of clever singers who cultivated the romance as we have already described it in the twelfth century. Representative of one of these was Quesnes de Bethune, a crusader and a famous warrior and diplomatist, who wrote both love poetry and satire ; of the other, Colin Muset, a poor trouvère who depended on his art for his bread. These writers for the most part wrote what are called *chansons*, which are much more like our notion of songs than the Chansons de Gestes. They are written in short stanzas, but without any very special arrangement of rhymes. Besides the singers already named, there were an immense number of others, known and unknown, some hundreds being counted by M. Paulin Paris, who had perhaps read more Old French literature than any man living or who ever lived. The most famous of all the lyric poets of

this century has however still to be mentioned. This is
Thibaut Count of Champagne and King of Navarre, the
earliest individual French poet who obtained by name
a considerable reputation even before the revival of the
study of Old French literature in the present century.
Thibaut de Champagne, as he is generally called, was not
a great poet, but he was a good one, and as it happened,
he is the central figure of a group of other noble poets,
who are certainly good if not great. Most of these are
little more than names to the modern reader, yet they
are of no little worth. Among them there is the Vidame
de Chartres, a great feudal personage who, like most others
of the time, went to the Crusades; and Hue de la Ferté, who
was a bitter enemy of Thibaut; and John of Brienne, King
of Jerusalem, who, like Quesnes de Bethune, was famous
not merely in song but in war and council ; and the Châtelain
de Coucy; and many more, too many to mention. (All
these great chiefs and nobles wrote verse, sometimes of
the love-poem kind, sometimes satirical and rather personal.
Thibaut was the best of them all.) He was not himself
a hero, like Quesnes de Bethune and King John of Brienne,
but he was a very important person in feudal France,
having great possessions both in the north and in the
south, between which parts of the country there was then
a strong and sharp division. He was not popular with his
contemporaries, perhaps because he assisted the mother of
St. Louis, Blanche of Castile, in maintaining the royal authority
in the sorely divided land. But his songs are very original,
very sweet, and very free from the monotony which is
the great drawback of mediæval literature. He was born
in 1201, and died in 1253, so that his life almost exactly
covers the first half of the thirteenth century, and must
have been contemporary with that of Marie de France,

whose precise date is however not known, though she certainly lived at the court of our Henry III. Thibaut's works are less extensive and less varied than Marie's, consisting as they do of some sixty or seventy songs only. But with her he has generally been ranked as representing early French lyric poetry. A wider knowledge has since discovered many other writers of equal if not superior talents, but it has not interfered with the interest attaching to the work of these two.

After Marie and Thibaut in the first part of the century, there are two other poets in the second part who deserve notice, one because he did what he did do extremely well, and the other because he was the first, as far as we know, to do some things of great importance. Rutebœuf(1230?–1290?) as the first was named, or nick-named, is a very good example of the later trouvère, who did not write long poems, was not a nobleman, nor directly attached to any noble house, and probably had on the whole a hard and unprosperous life. His poems are of very different kinds, but most of them are either satirical or religious. Rutebœuf wrote several fabliaux, and he is supposed to have written one of the divisions (though it is one of the worst) of the great *Roman du Renart.* He wrote a miracle-play too, and a life in verse of St. Elizabeth of Hungary, and another of St. Mary of Egypt. But perhaps his most interesting poems to us are the personal ones, in which he either deals with his own affairs or comments on the historical events of the time. The very titles of the former tell their own tale. They are 'The Complaint of Rutebœuf,' 'Rutebœuf's marriage,' and so forth, while the historical pieces are for the most part laments on celebrated persons who had died. These latter were most probably composed, as we should say, on commission for the survivors, and often include very interesting details. Thus the indignant phrase in one of the historical poems, 'mort sont Ogier et Charlemagne,' expresses excellently the decay of the earlier chivalry, and so do the many invectives made by the poet against the extinction of the crusading spirit in France.

Adam de la Halle (exact date uncertain: latter half of the century) is a less interesting person than Rutebœuf, and seems to have been a much more unamiable one. He has left a very spiteful contrast between the fondness he felt for his wife before he married her and the desire he felt to get away from her afterwards, and he has also represented his father in by no means a respectful or filial manner. But he is a decidedly important figure in the history of French literature, because, as far as we know, nobody before him had done what he did. Mystery and miracle-plays had been written for some time. Now it seems to have struck Adam that there was no reason why no other use should be made of the drama than this, and he accordingly wrote a play called _Li Jus Adam_, literally 'Adam's play,' in which he himself, his father, and many other citizens of Arras, his native town, are brought on the stage. This was, in short, the first French comedy. Adam did something else remarkable of the same kind. He took the common and popular pastour-elle of _Robin et Marion_ and made this into what we should now call an operetta, making the various personages speak and sing instead of merely telling their story himself as others had done before. Our knowledge of the literature of the time is not exact enough to enable us to say that these two things, comedy and comic opera, which Adam de la Halle had certainly produced some twenty years before the end of the thirteenth century, were his own invention. But nobody, as far as we know, had done a similar thing in a modern language before, and nobody did it again for many long years, though mysteries and miracle-plays, often with comic interludes, became more and more common. Thus Adam appears to be entitled to the credit—a very rare one in literary history—of having, as far as his own language was concerned, and with no direct aid from any other, actually invented two important literary forms, one of them destined to produce some of the very best works in French literature, and both peculiarly consonant to the genius of the nation. The fables which Marie wrote, and the fabliaux, of which some notice was given in the last chapter, and which were written more than ever in the thirteenth century, joined together to produce one of the most remarkable works of the middle ages, the *Roman du Renart,* or story of Reynard the Fox. This famous story, which has been translated into all the languages of Northern Europe, cannot be traced with certainty to any one original. Some people will have it that it was originally written in German, some in Northern French, some in Latin, some (and they seem to have most reason on their side) in French, but French of a decidedly Flemish kind. However this may be, most of the names of the beasts in the story are French, and the French poems on the subject are much the most remarkable as well as much the longest. Everybody knows the main outlines of the story, or rather the collection of stories, which bears the title. Reynard the Fox deceives and gets the better of all the other beasts by turns, though sometimes he is hard put to it, and his retreat or castle of Maupertuis is threatened. In the long French poem which goes under the title of *Roman du Renart* (it should be 'de Renart,' for this is a proper name), we have a great many different pieces by different authors, fastened together and making up in all a total of more than thirty thousand lines. Very few of the authors of these are known, and, except that the

personages of most of them are the same, they have little
connection the one with the other, each of them telling of
some separate trick of Reynard's. It has already been
noticed how fond the poets of the time were of taking up
and completing each other's work, so as to avoid the trouble
of inventing an entirely new subject, and *Renart* is a striking
example. Some of the poems of this the ' Ancien Renart,'
as it is called, may belong to the twelfth century, and few
of them are later than the first half of the thirteenth. Somewhere about the middle of this time a longer poem—that
is, longer than any of the divisions of the old story, though
not one tenth of the whole in length—was written, called *Le
Couronnement Renart*. In the old story, the Fox, though
frequently disobedient to King Noble, the Lion, and often
making a fool of him, is still outwardly loyal and respectful.
Here his success and daring go so far that he is actually
crowned king. It used to be thought that this poem was by
Marie de France, but there is no reason for this belief, and it
is not at all like her writing. Then, towards the end of the
century, one Jacquemart Giélée, a Fleming, wrote a long
poem called *Renart le Novel*, in some eight thousand lines.
This is much less amusing than the old stories, and is full
of rather tedious allegory and personification, things that
were invading French literature almost everywhere at this
time. And last of all (to finish with Renart while we are
about him), an immense poem called *Renart le Contrefait*
was written in the fourteenth century, which seems to have
still more moralising and digression in it, and still less story.
Renart le Contrefait has never been printed, and it is therefore difficult to judge it properly.

Good as was the general spirit and character of the literature of this time, the two drawbacks which have been noticed
in these continuations of *Renart* made themselves pretty

obvious as the century went on. (These drawbacks were, it
must be repeated, the tendency to allegory and to intro-
ducing abstract qualities as persons, and the tendency to
drag in all sorts of incongruous digressions and to make
occasions of showing what learned men the poets were.)
This was still more strikingly shown in the other great poem
of the century, the *Roman de la Rose.* This Roman de la
Rose has a very curious history, for it was written by two
different poets at a considerable distance of time. The
work of the first, Guillaume de Lorris, who lived before the
middle of the century, was an allegorical love-poem, full of
pretty descriptions of gardens and so forth. Guillaume tells
his readers how he fell asleep and dreamt that he came
under the walls of a fair garden whose walls were painted all
about with figures. These figures represent abstract virtues
or vices, or qualities of some kind or another, such as hypocrisy, pride, etc., and the personages thus represented, with
many others of the same kind, such as *Bel-acueil, Dangier,*
and the like, help or hinder the poet in his attempts to
gather the beautiful rosebud he has seen and fallen in love
with. When Guillaume de Lorris had written between four
and five thousand verses he seems to have been interrupted sud-
denly by death or some other cause. Forty years afterwards
another poet, called Jean Clopinel, or Jean de Meung, took
up the poem and finished it in a very different spirit. Instead of a graceful allegory about love (or rather besides
this, for the main design of the poem was nominally kept up)
Jean made it a satirical discussion of politics, morals, and
many other things, while he brought in all sorts of classical
quotations and miscellaneous stories to suit the taste of the
time. In this way, before he had finished he made it nearly
five times as long as Guillaume de Lorris had left it, and as
unlike in character as two things can well be. But the

poem became enormously popular, and remained so till the
end of the middle ages, and even much later. (Chaucer
translated a large part of it (though it is held by some that
the translation which now goes by his name is not that
which he wrote), and the imitations both in England and
France were numberless. Indeed for two hundred years at
least hardly anybody wrote a love-poem in either of the two
countries which was not in some degree an offspring of
the *Roman de la Rose.*) The writers never spoke straight-
forwardly and directly, but always in roundabout allegorical
phrase, often using the very allegory and personages of the
Rose. This was very bad, and makes such poetry very
tedious to read. But the *Roman de la Rose* itself is well
worth reading, and there is perhaps no other single work
which lets us see so clearly what the later middle ages
thought about science, politics, and many other things.

It would have been strange if, while poetry was thus
in many ways receiving development, prose had been
altogether behindhand. We have already mentioned some
prose works of the time, but the most important has yet
to be noticed. It was not till the end of the twelfth,
or perhaps the beginning of the thirteenth century, that the
most fertile of all branches of prose writing, history,
began to be cultivated in France in the vulgar tongue, and
even then writers for some time chiefly confined themselves
to translations. Collections of chronicles, written in Latin
and reduced to uniformity and continuity, had for some time
been growing common, and it was these, or parts of them,
that were first turned into French. For all this a writer of
genius showed himself almost as soon as the practice had
been begun. Geoffroy de Villehardouin was a noble of the
Province of Champagne, and bore a part in the Fourth
Crusade (1203). Of this Crusade (the great exploit of which

was not any victory over the infidels, but the capture of Constantinople and the establishment for rather more than half a century of a Latin Empire of the East) Villehardouin has left us an account, called *La Conquête de Constantinoble*, which probably gives to the reader a better idea of chivalry and feudalism at their best than any other single work. We find in it all the ardour, the picturesque colour, the love of fighting, and the apparently fervent piety, which distinguish the *Chansons de Gestes*, while at the same time the author does not for a moment attempt to conceal the self-seeking, the mutual jealousies, and the insubordination which were the great curses of the feudal system. Villehardouin was succeeded by Henri de Valenciennes and Robert de Clari. It is possible, though not certain, that the work of Henri was originally in rhyme, and that it was—according to a curious fashion of the time which shows the growing popularity of prose—'unrhymed,' as it was called; that is, turned into prose. This growing popularity is a very important thing in literary history, because it shows that the habit of reading was getting common. As long as the compositions of the trouvères were mainly recited, it was better to write them in verse, which was more attractive to the listeners, and easier for the reciter to remember. But when they began to be read there was no reason for writing them in any form more troublesome to the writer than prose. Still it was not till the latter end of the thirteenth century that what may be called the official history of France, the *Grandes Chroniques de St. Denis*, began to be written in the national language. By that time a second original writer of great importance had arisen. This was Jean de Joinville, the companion and historian of St. Louis. Joinville writes in quite a different style from Villehardouin; he is still, as we should expect, a brave knight and

experienced warrior, but he cares much less for what may
be termed the poetry of fighting. He is by no means
convinced that it is not better to stay at home and mind
business, than to go wandering about the world in search
of adventures. When he is on his travels too, he has
curiosity about the ways and manners of the countries he
visits, while nothing of the kind ever seems to occur to
Villehardouin. In accordance with these peculiarities the
later book is much less picturesque and poetical than the
earlier, but more easily written, fuller of interesting little
details, and altogether more modern. The interval of time
between the two works, and still more between the states
of feeling which they represent, is indeed considerable, for
Joinville was not born till at least ten years after Villehardouin's death (which occurred, it is believed, about 1213),
and did not write till he was a very old man. During this
interval it was still fashionable to compose chronicles in
verse, and one such chronicle, that of Philippe Mouskès,
is of value. Its literary merit is small, but its author has
abstracted many of the old chansons (which he takes to be
historic documents), and these abstracts are often very useful
to throw light on the lost parts of the Carlovingian legend.
Works of this kind however, whether verse or prose, cannot
be compared for a moment with those of Villehardouin and
Joinville, which rise altogether out of the class of ordinary
literature, and deserve notice not merely in connection with
the French middle ages, but for their own intrinsic merit.
Still the composition of prose chronicles naturally encouraged
the use of the form. Besides chronicles, and besides the
miscellaneous didactic writings already noticed—the most
important of which is the *Trésor* of Brunetto Latini (1266),
the master of Dante, an Italian, who, he tells us, wrote in
French expressly on account of its wide vogue and fitness

for the purpose—two other kinds of literature gave important employment to the prose-writer. The sermons of Maurice de Sully at the close of the twelfth century have been noticed. The establishment of the great orders of St. Dominic and St. Francis in the thirteenth gave a great impulse to vernacular preaching, and sermons became from this time a regular branch of French literature. The law too came in for its share of attention. Already there had been important collections of edicts and legal procedure, such as those of William the Conqueror and the *Coutumier de Normandie.* But in the thirteenth century Philippe de Navarre (1240?) and Jean d'Ibelin (1266?) elaborated from the old traditions and customs of the Frankish kingdom of Jerusalem the *Assises de Jérusalem,* the most important record in existence of purely feudal jurisprudence. Somewhat later Philippe de Beaumanoir (who has the repute of a poet as well as of a lawyer, having written two long romans d'aventure, *La Manekine* and *Jehan de Dammartin et Blonde d'Oxford,* besides shorter poems) produced in the *Coutumes de Beauvoisis* (1283) another extremely important work, both from the point of view of legal history and of French prose style. Henceforward it may be said that French prose, if not yet quite fitted for all sorts of literary work, had at any rate attempted almost all sorts, and in some at least had achieved notable successes.

Hitherto we have been wholly occupied with the literature of French proper, from a linguistic point of view; that is to say, with the literature of Northern France. During all the earlier middle ages there was a very sharp division between French and what we now generally call Provençal, and between the people who spoke the two languages. The geographical boundary line was drawn, speaking roughly, from Poitou to Franche Comté, and the Provençal district

included, besides all the country of modern France to the
south of that line, Savoy beyond the Alps and Catalonia
beyond the Pyrenees. For a time this district had been
much harassed by the Saracens of Spain, but after Charles
Martel's great victory and the strong rule of Charlemagne, it
enjoyed for many centuries a much quieter government and
a more advanced social civilisation than Northern France.
The eastern part of it, under the powerful Counts of
Toulouse, the western under the Dukes of Aquitaine and
the Kings of England, were prosperous and flourishing,
while the northern provinces were torn first by the northern
invasions and then by the feudal dissensions of the great
vassals. The language too of this part of the country was
somewhat 'earlier suitable for literary performances. It
altered less from the Latin, and was on the whole more like
Spanish or Italian than French. (The vowel-terminations
which are characteristic of southern tongues remained in it,
and made rhyme and complicated poetical forms easy.) We
have mentioned a poem on Boethius which is of the tenth
century, and which shows far more literary capacity in the
language than the contemporary song of St. Eulalia in
Northern French. There was however a very remarkable
deficiency of inventiveness in those who spoke the Southern
dialect to balance their greater advantages in point of
language. It does not appear that the Chansons de Gestes
had any representatives in early times in Provençal, or if they
had any they were merely translated or imitated from the
French, in the dialect nearest to that language. Provence
lay far from Brittany, and it was long before the attractive
and stimulating legend of Arthur penetrated to the shores
of the Mediterranean. The Provençals indeed seem to have
had little genius for story-telling, narrative or dramatic. One
of the earliest specimens of dramatic work that we have in

French, the mystery of the _Ten Virgins_, is in a language which is almost as much Provençal as French, showing that at the time and in the place of its composition the two dialects had not fully separated, yet Provençal has but little if anything to show in the mystery way afterwards. Against all these deficiencies, however, has to be set a remarkable and almost unparalleled fertility in lyrical poetry. Provence, in the wide sense we have indicated, was the country of the troubadours, and for two centuries the troubadours set the example to Europe in the point of lyric verse. They were extraordinarily numerous, and they received extraordinary encouragement in the somewhat artificial style of love-poetry which they principally but not solely affected. The longer works of Provençal literature which have much merit are very few. _Girartz de Rossilho_ (Gérard de Roussillon), the one Chanson de Geste which seems to have been originally written in a Southern dialect; the celebrated poem, on the Albigensian Crusade, written at the time of the events by two different poets of very unequal merit; the interesting romance of _Flamenca_, possessing unusual attraction as a study of character and manners; and that of _Jaufre_, a good Roman d'Aventures, almost exhaust the list. On the other hand, the number of the troubadours proper, that is to say the lyric poets, is very large; the names of nearly five hundred have come down to us, and their work is both abundant and various. They began to write or sing at the end of the eleventh century, and their palmy time was the twelfth and the earlier part of the thirteenth. By the end of this latter century literature in Provence, even more than in Northern France, had passed into a condition of decadence. These troubadours, like the northern trouvères, were of all conditions, but knights and nobles, even great princes, made up a very large proportion of their numbers. Assisted

by the frequent vowel-sounds and melodious cadences of
the language they devised many artificial forms of verse,
the rules of which were extremely complicated and precise.
The subjects dealt with were, however, very few, being
chiefly love, war, and, to a certain extent, personal satire;
and the different classes of poem were designated by names
sometimes referring to their form, sometimes to their matter.
Thus there were the *alba,* a morning greeting or farewell, as
the case might be; the *serena,* or serenade; the *sirvente,*
generally a satiric poem; the *planh,* or complaint; the *tenson*
(contention), in which two singers dispute with one another;
the *ensenhamen,* or didactic poem. Of the species named,
from their form may be mentioned the *canson,* the chief
form for love-poems, and very elaborate in construction;
the *balada,* which, like the Northern *ballade,* had a refrain
but was less regular in form; the *retroenza,* of somewhat
similar nature; the *descort,* in which the metre and rhymes
of each stanza were different; and finally the *sestina,* which
is perhaps the most complicated of all. So numerous are
the troubadours that it is hard even to select names here.
The most famous perhaps, partly for their poetry, partly
for stories more or less romantic connected with their lives,
are Bertran de Born, the warlike accomplice of the disobedient
sons óf our Henry II; Guillem de Cabestanh, the hero of
a well-known story of barbarous revenge; Jaufre Rudel,
celebrated for his love of the lady of Tripoli, at whose feet,
having at last come to sight and speech of her, he died;
Peire Vidal, an eccentric person (who on one occasion
dressed himself up as a wolf, and roamed about thus attired
in honour of his beloved, whose name was 'Loba'—she-
wolf) but a very good poet; Sordello, whom Dante and
Mr. Browning have helped to make famous; Folquet, who
lived to be something very different from a troubadour;

Guillem de Figueiras, author of a terrible poetical attack on Rome and her corruptions. But of many little or nothing is known, and some of the most beautiful poems (especially an alba beginning *en un vergier soiz folha d'albespi*, which is typical of the whole literature) are anonymous.

From this sketch of the thirteenth-century literature of France it will be obvious that, such as it was, it had reached its zenith. Nothing better of the kind could be done than the Chansons de Gestes, the Arthurian stories, and the Romans d'Aventures, the Fabliaux, and the Roman du Renart and the Roman de la Rose, the romances of Audefroy and Thibaut, the satirical and personal poems of Rutebœuf and Adam de la Halle. What these things wanted was precisely what they could not have without a complete change in the language and the thought, and the persons who wrote and read or heard them. Consequently, in the remaining years of the middle ages—there were nearly a hundred and fifty of them—we hear nothing absolutely new in French literature. (Some few things of the old kinds are done better than they were before; additional attention to the minutiæ of form and language results in work of a more elegant kind than is previously to be discovered, and a few writers of great genius single themselves out from the mass, as writers of great genius always will do.) But until the Renaissance no general period of literary excellence occurs, and when the next period of general literary excellence does occur, the conditions, the stock in trade, and the objects of literary work are entirely changed. The reasons for this comparatively sudden decadence are partly political, depending on the decay of feudalism and the English wars. With these we are not concerned. But there were not a few causes of a purely literary kind also at work. The immense popularity which the allegorical matter of the Roman de la Rose and the artificial manner—to be noticed in the next chapter—of writing lyric poetry attained, made it easy for writers to go on simply producing new work of the old kind. Nor were the language and the stock of general ideas and subjects of thought as yet fitted for a new kind of writing. There was, as has been pointed out, considerable knowledge of the classics among a few scholars, but it was for the most part limited to the Latin classics, and it was wholly confined to a few learned men, and could not be well extended until the invention of printing and the complete break-up of the mediæval polity in Church and State had altered social conditions. A great many of the literary exercises of the period on which we shall now enter may be fairly enough compared to the exercises of chivalry, which like them long continued to be popular. They had lost the real practical importance and life which they had once possessed. But they were suitable enough to the tastes of the persons who pursued them; they were graceful and interesting in themselves, and the time was not ready for the substitution of anything else. Hence, though there is much that is interesting in the literature of the fourteenth and fifteenth centuries, it is with justice that the thirteenth is regarded as the palmy time of mediæval letters in France, the time when the old language was in its chief vigour, and was handled by the greatest number of writers of individual genius and talent.

CHAPTER III.

As has been already pointed out at the conclusion of the last chapter, there is, after the first few years of the fourteenth century, a decided falling off in the quality of French literature, and in the number of good authors who contributed to it. This was due to a great many causes, of which the rapid decay of the feudal system was not the least. France fell into a state of great disorganisation, and during what is called the Hundred Years War people had something else to do than to think and write. Still there is much that is interesting to be found by those who look for it. The *Chansons de Gestes* almost ceased to be written, though a few of them were extended and magnified in the taste of the time, and one very remarkable one was composed. This is entitled *Bauduin de Sebourc,* and is in all probability, with its sequel *Le Bastart de Buillon*, the very latest original poem of the kind which was ever written. It is connected with the *Geste* or series of the Crusades, and it tells the adventures of the hero not merely in the Holy Land but in Europe, where he has to fight with the enemies of his house. But it is not the adventures of *Bauduin de Sebourc,* though they are very interesting, that give it its peculiar value. It is the spirit in which it was written. It is in parts rather a satire than an epic, and it tells of a complete change in the general way of

regarding life and its affairs. Towards the end of the fourteenth century Chansons de Gestes in verse ceased to be
written altogether, and began to be translated into prose, in
which state they still continued to be popular with readers—
for the old institution of recitations had nearly died out.
The same was the case with the Arthurian romances. But
the Romans d'Aventures, which had no peculiar or common
subject, continued to be produced in some numbers, and
short prose stories began to be popular, such as those of
which we have already heard in the last chapter.

A change likewise came over the nature of smaller and
lighter poems. There were many poets who wrote such
things, the chief of them being in the fourteenth century,
Jean de Lescurel (? before 1350), Guillaume de Machault
(1295?–1380?), Eustache Deschamps (1328–1415), and Jean
Froissart (1333–1410); with Alain Chartier (1386–1458),
Christine de Pisan (1363–1420), Charles d'Orléans (1391–
1465), François Villon (1431–   ?), and Guillaume Coquillart (?–1510) in the fifteenth. The longer poems of these
men (with the exception of Villon) are chiefly allegorical
love-poems, something in the style of the *Roman de la Rose*,
not so long indeed, but far more tedious. (Their shorter
poems are much more serious and interesting.) They are
written in certain forms or arrangements, in which the number of the lines and rhymes is the same for all the stanzas,
and does not differ in each as is usual. The sonnet, which
consists of fourteen lines with the rhymes arranged in a
regular order, is the only poem of this kind that has, till
lately, been much written in English. The sonnet is an
Italian invention, and the French poets of the fourteenth and
fifteenth century did not write it. But instead they wrote
ballades and *rondeaux*. (The ballade was a poem of three
stanzas. It might have from six to ten lines each, but the

last line was always the same, and so were the rhymes in
each stanza, while the poem was often finished off with
what was called *l'envoy*, an address in four lines to some
person, real or imagined, and ending like the other stanzas
with the refrain.) Eustache Deschamps wrote more than
a thousand such ballads. The rondeau, which had some
subordinate kinds, known as the rondel, the triolet, &c.,
was a much shorter poem, in which the first words of the
first line—in the rondel and triolet the first line, or two lines,
—were repeated at intervals. These repetitions give a very
musical sound when they are well managed, but sometimes
they are dragged in without much sense or aptness, and
then the poems are dull enough. Guillaume de Machault
wrote many other kinds of verse, and led a stirring life.
He was attached at one time to the old blind King of
Bohemia, who was killed at Cressy, at another to Pierre de
Lusignan, King of Cyprus, one of the last of the errant
kings whom the Crusades had established in the East.
When Machault was quite an old man he fell in love
with Agnes of Navarre (or perhaps with another lady, for
it is not certain), and a curious poem called the *Voir Dit*—
true tale—tells the story. Eustache Deschamps, besides
his ballades and rondeaux and other short poems, wrote an
'Art of Poetry,' to teach other people how to write them,
a long poem called the *Mirror of Marriage*, in the moralising and allegorical taste of the time, and other works, which
amount in all to more than 80,000 verses. (Froissart, who
is more famous as a historian, wrote poems of the same
sort, which fill three thick volumes.) Besides these there
were many anonymous poets. An interesting book called
Le Livre des Cent Ballades was the joint composition, it is
thought, of several gentlemen who were making a voyage to
the East, with Bouciqualt, the Marshal of France, who was

afterwards captured at Agincourt, at their head. Christine de Pisan and Alain Chartier were still more inclined to moralising in their verse. But in Charles d'Orléans we come to the best writer by far of this kind of poetry. Charles was the son of that Duke of Orleans who was murdered in the streets of Paris by the Burgundians, and his youth was spent amid the quarrels which then distracted France. He too was taken at Agincourt, where he held high command in the French army, and he was kept prisoner in England for many years. When he went back to France he was wiser and lazier, and took but little part in public affairs, but gathered a great body of minstrels and men of letters at his castle of Blois, and spent the time, like King René of Anjou later, in rhyming and singing. His verses tell us how he had vowed himself to the service of the *Dieu Nonchaloir*, the god of indifference, and in fact when he tries to be earnest his poetry is not worth much. But his little rondels about the seasons, about his love affairs (mostly fancy ones), and so forth, are among the best poetry of the kind that has ever been written. A very different poet was Villon, who lived a vagabond and disreputable life, and has left strange poems called *Testaments*, in which, under guise of bequeathing his different possessions, he tells us all his life, and satirises his friends and enemies alike. These poems are studded here and there with ballades and rondeaux, so full of sad and beautiful poetry, that even those who care for no other mediæval work admit their charm. One of Villon's ballades is on ' The Ladies of Past Time.' It is little more than a list of names, with the burden *Mais où sont les neiges d'antan* (where are the snows of last year?), but the note of regret and passion is true and sweet, as only the best poetry is or can be. Coquillart was not so good a poet, but a very good

satirist, and somewhere about this time there lived in
Normandy a miller, Olivier Basselin by name, whose pa-
triotic and convivial songs got a great vogue. It is not
certain that we have any of them, though it is possible.
Later in the century there were no good poets, but people
went on writing stiff ballades and rondeaux, making
the rules more and more difficult, as if by so doing they
could make the poetry better. Unluckily there is no such
easy way of securing good poets.

As the poetry however, with some brilliant exceptions, continued to get worse and worse, so the prose continued to get
better and better. We have seen that, by the end of the thirteenth century, men had quite got over the idea that French
prose was not suitable for the treatment of serious subjects.
They still, however, were rather inclined to write in verse
when they wanted to secure an audience, no matter what the
subject might be. In the time we are now handling, this
custom began to grow out of fashion. It became quite usual
to write history in French, and to the fourteenth century belongs Froissart, who has probably been more read than any
other French author before the invention of printing. Froissart was a Hainaulter by birth, and was much patronised by
Queen Philippa of England. He spent nearly his whole life
in journeying about from court to court, and picking up news
about the battles and other events of the time. His poems,
of which we have already spoken, were mostly the work of
his youth; his history, of his middle life and old age. At
first he began by closely copying the *Chroniques* of Jean
Lebel, Canon of Liège, but this part of his work he
altered a good deal in what we should now call later editions.
At first he was very much on the English side, but in this
too he changed latterly to some extent. In fact we do not
go to Froissart for opinions, or even for a very trustworthy

statement of historical facts, but for brilliant descriptions of striking events. In this last respect hardly any historian has ever surpassed him, and his book is as delightful as any romance. It became very popular, and decided no doubt a great many other people to write French histories, though in this same century we have a last survival of the old practice, in the shape of a long poem written like a Chanson de Geste, on the great Breton hero Duguesclin and his achievements. Froissart was continued by Monstrelet, a rather dull writer, and by many others whose names are hardly worth mentioning. In the memoirs of Marshal Bouciqualt, we have a book much more in Froissart's own style. Soon too people began to attend to things to which Froissart had paid little attention, because they concerned not kings and queens, and knights and ladies, but citizens and poor people. Juvenal des Ursins (1388–1473), who wrote a long history of the disastrous reign of Charles VI, puts down all sorts of minute facts, which are not perhaps of much importance individually, but which help better than anything else to give us an idea of the actual state of the country, and of its daily life. Of the same sort are some very interesting journals of anonymous 'Citizens of Paris,' which give us an account, from the Burgundian side, of the terrible struggles between that party and the Armagnacs, and the history of Jean de Troyes, called the *Chronique scandaleuse*, which deals with the reign of Louis the Eleventh. Last of all, and finishing our period, is another famous book, as remarkable as Froissart's, though in a different way, the memoirs of Philippe de Comines (1445–1509). Comines was a statesman, who first served Charles the Bold of Burgundy, then Louis the Eleventh, and lastly Charles the Eighth. He is just the opposite of Froissart. He does not describe battles well, nor indeed is he good at description of any kind. But he pays a great deal of attention to the causes of things and to their political aspects, so that his book has been called the first philosophical history of modern Europe.

It has been said that at this time prose fiction began to be written more commonly. ⸀At first it took the form either of short tales or of prose adàptations of the verse romances.⸣ But soon writers grew bolder. There is a delightful little story called *Jean de Paris*, the date of which is uncertain, which no Englishman can help enjoying, though the butt of the story is an English king. The hero is the king of France, who disguises himself under the title of ' John of Paris.' But the most famous prose writer of fiction during the latter part of our time was Antoine de la Salle (1398–1461). It is thought that he was the author of three prose works, each of which is a masterpiece. The first is a romance called *Petit Jean de Saintré.* This tells how a young knight of that name was chosen by a beautiful lady as her lover and servant, how he gained great renown for bravery and courtesy, how he went away to fight the infidels, and in his absence she preferred to him a rich abbot, so that when he came back he exposed her faithlessness before the court. The lady is called by the curious title of 'La Dame des Belles Cousines.' This book is a very pleasant sketch of the better side of chivalry, as it was in fancy rather than in fact, for the reality had departed before La Salle's time. Another work believed to be his is even more famous. This is the *Cent Nouvelles Nouvelles*, clever prose versions of the old fabliau stories supposed to have been told before the Dauphin, afterwards Louis the Eleventh, when he was living at Genappe under the protection of Philip of Burgundy. The last of the three is called *Les Quinze Joyes du Mariage*, and is a bitter satire upon women. These three books together give an almost complete view of the good and bad side of society in the later middle ages, and they are extremely well written. The *Cent Nouvelles Nouvelles* especially is one of the earliest works of polished French prose.

Besides history and prose fiction a great deal of other prose work was done. The *Castoiements*, or moral treatises in verse, of which we have spoken, gave way to prose books of the same kind. One of the earliest and best of these is the book which the Chevalier de la Tour Landry wrote for the instruction of his daughters. It consists of a number of short chapters, often with stories in them illustrative of right and wrong conduct. The evils of the Hundred Years War also caused a good deal of serious prose work to be written. Christine de Pisan wrote a life of Charles V, which was nominally a biography, but in reality rather a treatise of advice to his successors. Alain Chartier, too, wrote several moral and political treatises. These authors, and others, such as Raoul de Presles and Nicholas Oresme, also undertook the very important work of translating the classics into French. This enriched the language with a great many new words, which were however not always very well chosen, and give the books in which they occur something of a pedantic look.

About this time sermons began to play a very important part in literature and in history. During the thirteenth century, it will be remembered, it became common to write sermons in French, and as the political struggles of the different princes and parties in France grew hotter, it became more and more important for each in turn to secure so important an engine of persuasion as the pulpit. Even such acts as the murder of the Duke of Orleans found defenders among the clergy. About the middle of the fifteenth century several preachers of great note arose, of whom the chief were Raulin (1443–1514), Menot (1450–1518), and Maillard (1440–1502). These men did not observe what we should now call decency in the pulpit; they told comic stories, and used vulgar and even blasphemous language, besides addressing their audiences much more personally than would now be endured. But they were on the whole well-meaning and fearless in the denunciation of abuses, and those of their sermons which survive throw great light on the social conditions of the day. The greatest name of our present period in respect of preaching and of theological literature, is however an earlier one, that of Jean Gerson (1363–1429), Chancellor of the University of Paris, to whom (on insufficient evidence) the authorship of the *Imitation of Christ* has sometimes been assigned. Gerson was a good preacher, and his sermons both in Latin and French exist in considerable numbers. The latter are well-written and arranged, though they suffer occasionally from the drawback almost universal at this time of excessive and wearisome allegory.

While prose was thus advancing to perfection, and while poetry proper was showing evidences of gradual decline, a form of literary work which for the most part stands between prose and poetry, the drama, was flourishing in various peculiar and characteristic ways. It had begun in France, as we have seen, with dramas or mysteries of a liturgical kind in the twelfth and thirteenth centuries, while in the latter, Adam de la Halle had laid the foundation of purely secular dramatic work. During the troubles of the fourteenth century it does not appear that Adam's example was followed. But a new kind of sacred dramatic work, the miracle-play, seems to have acquired popularity. The miracle-play is distinguished from the mystery because it connects itself less closely with the Scriptures and the

services of the Church, and embodies, for the most part,
various apocryphal legends about the saints and the Virgin.
The most remarkable monument of this kind of literature
is a manuscript in the Paris National Library, which contains
forty miracles of the Virgin Mary. (These plays average
about fifteen hundred lines in length, and tell of all sorts
of incidents in which the Virgin helped her devotees.) They
seem, as far as can be made out from the manuscript, to
have been performed by a kind of club or society which met
together for the purpose, and which bore the title of *Puy
Notre Dame.* These *Puys* were not infrequent institutions
of the middle ages in France, and in the days before acting
became a profession they generally undertook the performance of dramas. By degrees other societies were
formed, and undertook the representation of a very large
number of different kinds of dramatic work. The fifteenth
century is exceedingly rich in such societies and in their
productions. In the first place the old mystery-plays,
which had generally been busied with some short portion
of the Scriptures or the Church Service, were connected
together, rewritten in the taste of the time, and made into
huge dramas, the acting of which sometimes took up as
much as four or five weeks. The best-written and most
famous of these is the mystery of the Passion (before 1452),
by Arnould Gréban, which is 35,000 lines in length. Simon
Gréban, brother of the author, wrote *Actes des Apôtres* to
complete it, and the two were connected and lengthened
still further by a certain Michel. Then there is a great
Mistère du Viel Testament which is about 50,000 lines
long, and of which the author is unknown. So popular
did these vast compositions become, that 'profane' mysteries
as they were called were written on the same plan. The old
romance of Troy was turned into a mystery, and the siege

of Orleans, in which Joan of Arc figured, was treated in the same way very soon after its date. To act the sacred mysteries a 'Confraternity of the Passion' was founded at Paris in 1402, and no doubt similar bodies existed in provincial towns.

It was not likely that when acting and playgoing were both so fashionable, sacred subjects or heavy historical pieces should monopolise the stage, and very soon other companies were formed to play lighter pieces. These pieces were called *moralities, soties, farces, sermons joyeux,* and *monologues.* And the companies which played them were the 'Clercs de la Basoche' (the law-clerks and law-students of Paris), the 'Enfants sans souci' (a body of young men of respectable birth who amused themselves in this way), and several other societies with quaint titles. The morality was only by comparison lighter than the mysteries. It was doubtless a result of the passion for allegorical poetry which has been noticed, and it brought on the stage all sorts of personified virtues and vices, and even stranger figures than these. Sometimes the moralities were nearly as long as the great mysteries, but as a rule they are much more moderate in dimensions. A good example is the 'Condemnation of Banquet,' Banquet being a personified instance of gluttony and extravagance. The play opens with a wise speech by a kind of chorus, then 'Banquet' with 'Dinner,' 'Supper,' 'Gluttony,' etc., is introduced, together with a great many diseases, who threaten him with the consequences of his excess. Nevertheless there is a joyous feast, and Banquet mocks the diseases, while the chorus (Doctor Prolocutor he is called) draws the moral. Then the catastrophe approaches, the diseases attack the guests and kill them all, while Banquet is finally put to death for tempting them. As the morality was a moral play, and the mystery and miracle

religious ones, so the sotie was chiefly political, and under
the figure of some stock characters, 'Le Prince des Sots,'
'Mère Sotte,' etc., occasion was taken to satirise abuses or
obnoxious things and persons in church and state. This, in
the condition of things at the time, could only be done under
powerful protection, and so the sotie was the least frequent
of all the kinds. The farce, on the contrary, was the most
frequent of all. It was for the most part a putting into
dramatised dialogue of the old merry adventures recounted
in the fabliaux, and was evidently immensely popular. About
a hundred and fifty farces have been preserved, most of
which are of the end of the fifteenth or the very early
sixteenth century. Sometimes the farce had only one actor,
and in this case it was called a sermon joyeux or monologue,
though the actor, as in modern times, sometimes managed
to represent more than one person by changing his dress
and disguising his voice. An excellent example of the
monologue is that called *Le Franc Archer de Bagnolet*
(sometimes ascribed to Villon), in which the hero, a boastful
but cowardly soldier, takes a scarecrow by the roadside for
an adversary, and manifests abject poltroonery. The sermons
joyeux, as their name implies, were most frequently parodies
of the curious discourses usual in the pulpit at the time, but
applied to secular subjects. But both of these styles were
far inferior in importance to the farce proper, which may
have any number of personages, and is in every respect a
complete comedy on a small scale. The most famous of all
these performances (sometimes nowadays ascribed to Antoine
de la Salle) is that of *Pathelin*, which is known to every
student of French from the adaptation of it made by Brueys
and Palaprat, in the seventeenth century. All the best of
the fun is in the original version. Another extremely clever
farce is that called *Le Cuvier*, where a henpecked husband

is made to sign a long list of duties, which he engages
himself to perform without murmuring, for his wife. Soon
afterwards the wife overbalances herself and falls into a large
washing-tub. In vain she implores her husband to pull her
out. *Ceci n'est pas dans mon rollet*—'It is not in the bond'—
is all she can get out of him. There is one very curious
thing about these farces, which is noticeable also in some of
the other dramatic forms, and which shows how strong a
hold the artificial forms of verse described at the beginning
of the chapter had obtained on the popular taste. The
characters frequently speak in triolets or short rondeaux,
repeating the lines so as to complete the form between them.
It has been thought that these farces were acted, like the
Greek satiric plays, after more serious dramas, and in some
cases it is known that this was the fact, but it cannot be said
with certainty that it was a general rule. They are however
for the most part so short that, except at fairs and suchlike
entertainments, it is difficult to imagine that they can have
formed the whole of the performance. No division of old
French literature, with the possible exception of the fabliaux,
shows more clearly the bent of the national genius and the
inexhaustible store of wit of a certain practical kind which
the lower classes possessed. For these entertainments are
evidently intended for the most part rather as amusements
for these classes than for their superiors. They continued
to be fashionable for a very long time, and even Molière's
earliest works were in very nearly the same style as the old
farces of the fifteenth and sixteenth century, most of which
have only recently been made available for study. The best
collection of them was found by accident in Germany some
forty years ago, and is now in the British Museum.

CHAPTER IV.

THE RENAISSANCE.

ALTHOUGH the literature of the fifteenth century in France is not in itself of the greatest importance, and though it was marked by many signs of decadence, yet, side by side with these, there may be noted in it other signs pointing to a new growth of letters. The great movement which is called the Renaissance, and which resulted mainly, though not wholly, from the recurrence to Greek and Roman literature and art as models, was working in Italy throughout the century, and the close connection between French and Italians resulting from the wars of Charles VIII and Louis XII was certain to spread its influence northwards. Independently of this, the studies of native Frenchmen pointed in the same direction. Moreover, in the fifteenth-century literature of France are to be found other promising signs. In the works of Antoine de la Salle satire assumed a wider range and a more polished tone than in those of the fabliau writers. The passion for dramatic compositions, which enabled spectators to sit out mysteries that took weeks in the performance, was the certain forerunner of a great development of this class of literature. The gradual disuse of the allegorical fashion of love-poetry promised something more personal and genuine in this direction as in others, the discovery of new countries promoted a general spirit

of adventure and enquiry in intellectual as well as com-
mercial matters, the invention of printing gave an otherwise
impossible opportunity to this spirit; and lastly, the great
religious revolution of which Erasmus was the forerunner
and Luther the author, gave the amplest exercise to men's
powers of speaking and writing. From the very first the
Reformers fought the battle of the vernacular against the
learned tongues both as a matter of religious belief and of
worldly prudence, for it was by the use of the vernacular
that they gained adherents. In France especially the literary influence of the Reformation was immense, and it would
hardly be too much to say that the *Psalms* of Marot and the
Institution of Calvin set for the first time the example of
works destined to exercise a wide popular influence in
French verse and in French prose.

Clément Marot (1497–1544), who has just been mentioned,
is the first writer who deserves to be noticed in this division
of our subject. The son of a father of Norman extraction
(himself a poet), he was born in the south of France, at
Cahors, and the union of northern blood and southern birth
should not be overlooked in estimating his character and
that of his work. His earlier poems were of the *rhétoriqueur*
fashion[1], and the chief thing noticeable about them is the
pretty title *L'Adolescence Clémentine* (a reminiscence perhaps of
the *Chansons Georgines* of Georges Chastellain), under which
they were afterwards collected. Marot's father had been a
follower of the court, and he himself soon became a favourite
at that of Francis I, where he was one of the chief literary
lovers of Marguerite d'Angoulême, queen of Navarre, the
king's sister, and a great patroness of literature as well as of

---

[1] *Les Rhétoriqueurs* is a term often applied to the pedantic and
artificial writers of the 15th century, of whom Georges Chastellain
and Guillaume Crétin were the chief.

E

the new religious doctrines. Before long, however, the favour
with which these doctrines had from political reasons been
regarded at the French court, was (also for political reasons)
changed into persecution. The influence of Marguerite was
not in all cases able to save her favourites from their fate, and
Marot had to fly to Geneva and Italy. His poetical works
are of a very miscellaneous character, embracing almost all
the poetic forms which had been popular in the middle
ages, sometimes with a slight change, as of the *dit* into the
blason, and of the *fatrasie*, or nonsense-verse, into the *coq-
a-l'âne*. But it was not in the selection of the form, so much
as in the management of it, that Marot's peculiar talent lay.
Discarding the pedantic language and phrase of the rhétoriqueurs, and with it for the most part the apparatus of
allegorical personages which had been part of a poet's equipment for two centuries, he affected a singularly plain and
straightforward, but at the same time singularly graceful and
elegant fashion of diction. The simplicity and directness
which have ever since been characteristic of all but a few of
the best French authors, date to a great extent from Marot.
His translated psalms were extremely popular, and were said
to have done not a little to spread the reformed doctrines in
France, though this is probably a mistake. Around Marot
grew up a very numerous school of poets, some of whom
opposed him, while others regarded him as a master, though
almost all copied as well as they could his manner of writing.
The chief of these secondary poets was Mellin or Merlin de
Saint Gelais (1486-1558) who, like Marot, came of a
poetical family. Saint Gelais has the credit of being the first
to introduce into French the regular Italian sonnet, the most
famous and fortunate of all artificial forms of verse.

Marot however, though in many ways a representative of
the newer time, did not represent it fully, and in particular

did not express the reverence for classical antiquity which was the strongest of all its intellectual peculiarities, stronger even than the striving for religious and philosophical liberty. Indeed the peculiar bent of his taste, and his reaction against the pedantries of the rhétoriqueurs, inclined him rather in the opposite direction. Before the century was half past a second school of poetry was therefore set on foot, by an association of friends who were all ardent admirers of the classics, and who endeavoured, as nearly as might be, to shape French poetry and the French language on classical models. The chief of these were the celebrated Pléiade, a group of seven writers, whose names were Ronsard, Du Bellay, Baif, Jodelle, Daurat, Belleau, and Pontus de Tyard. Of these, Daurat was one of the oldest, and the instructor of the others in classical lore. Jodelle (1532–1573) was before all things a dramatic writer, and has the glory of writing *Cléopâtre*, the first regular French tragedy on the antique plan, and the first regular French comedy, *Eugène*. The models were Seneca and Terence rather than Sophocles and Aristophanes, but the style was suited to the taste of the people before whom it was set, and French tragedy followed no other for nearly three hundred years. The other five members of the Pléiade were chiefly poets, though Joachim du Bellay (1525–1560) was an eloquent and forcible writer of prose. Some of his smaller poems, such as those 'Ruins of Rome' which Spenser translated, the charming *Vanneur* or song of the winnower, and the *Sonnets to Olive*, are very beautiful. But the representative poet of the school is Pierre de Ronsard (1524–1585), who was its acknowledged head, and was for a very long time hailed as the 'prince of poets' both by Frenchmen and foreigners. The best works of Ronsard are his sonnets and his odes, in the latter of which his endeavour was to imitate Horace. All these poets, indeed, sought to classicise themselves as much as was possible. They brought into French Latin words by the hundred, and endeavoured even to naturalise the compound phrases of the Greek, though the genius of the French is wholly repugnant thereto. Yet the Pléiade as a whole is singularly free from the heaviness and dryness which have generally attended imitations of the classics in modern tongues. The truth was that, though its members professed to despise the middle ages, and even such modernised representatives of those ages as the followers of Marot, they were still themselves animated by a large portion of the mediæval and romantic spirit. The union of this with the classical attention to elegance and form, produced the various schools of art and literature to which the term Renaissance has been attached, and among which French sixteenth-century literature, and in particular the poetry of the Pléiade, hold an honourable place. Around the seven chiefs were grouped many minor writers, some of whom were superior to the stars of the Pléiade itself, with the exception of Ronsard and Du Bellay. Such were Jacques Tahureau (1527–1555), a charming writer of poetic trifles, who died very young; such Olivier de Magny (d. 1560), a more prolific but also short-lived bard; such Louise Labé (b. 1526), a poetess of Lyons.

But the two most famous of the followers of the Pléiade, though in some sort rebellious followers, were Du Bartas and D'Aubigné. (Both of these were eager Protestants, whereas the members of the Pléiade were either free-thinkers or attached more or less loosely to the established religion. Guillaume du Bartas (1544–1590) attempted works on a much greater scale than his predecessors, and was much more successful—for the *Franciade*, Ronsard's only long work, is anything but a success. The *Divine Sepmaine*, or Week of Creation, of Du Bartas, is an elaborate poem, containing much apocryphal natural history after the taste of the time, and written in phraseology of the stiffest Pléiade pattern; full of Latinisms, double epithets, and so forth, but at the same time abounding in passages of great eloquence and sustained dignity of language. The same may be said of his less-known works. Du Bartas, partly perhaps from partisan motives, was at one time exalted above Ronsard by popular taste, and he continued for a considerable time to be widely read in France, and by means of Sylvester's translation in England. Agrippa d'Aubigné (1550-1630) was a writer of a different character. (An ardent politician and Calvinist, his temper was haughty and rough, and led him to write satire rather than milder kinds of poetry.) *Les Tragiques* are among the first satires really deserving the name in French. They exhibit the true spirit of Juvenal, and are written in Alexandrine verse of admirable quality. (This metre, which had during the later middle ages shared the position of honour in poetry with the decasyllable, was now definitely accepted as the only medium for serious verse of the highest kind, both narrative and dramatic.) Jodelle's first play, the *Cléopâtre*, is partly written in Alexandrines, partly in decasyllables, but his second, *Didon*, is entirely in the former; and from that time forward the practice never varied. In the same way Ronsard's *Franciade* was the last serious poem of importance written in the decasyllable. *La Divine Sepmaine* and *Les Tragiques* established the use of the Alexandrine.

There was even more for the sixteenth century to do in respect of French prose than of French verse, and even more was actually done. Some of the greatest names in prose writing date from this period, and their work is, in many respects, still a model of style, though they themselves had hardly any predecessors by whom to guide their

attempts. Up to the beginning of the century, the only works
of importance that had been written in prose were chronicles,
and latterly, lengthy prose versions of the old verse
romances. A few sermons, a few legal works, a few short
prose tales, and still fewer treatises on serious subjects,
summed up the contents of French prose literature. Before
the close of the period, however, there was not a single
branch of literature practised in the present day, if we except
the comparatively recent growth of journalism, which had not
been attempted by writers of the first talent. The two
earliest prose works of importance were singularly different
in character, for they were the *Gargantua* and *Pantagruel* of
François Rabelais (1495?–1553), and the *Institution Chrétienne*
of Jean Calvin (1509–1564). Rabelais was a monk who
had left the cloister, who had given himself to the study of
medicine, and who was deeply imbued in all the learning,
literary and scientific, of the time. The tendency to a
peculiar variety of free-thinking, which has always been
strongly developed in the French character, and which
shows itself in a kind of sceptical ridicule of established
beliefs and institutions rather than in an earnest and
practical desire for reform, was eminently present in Rabelais.
His great work, so far as it has any form at all, has that of a
prose Roman d'Aventures, and probably borrowed some at
least of its personages from popular works already in
existence. The story however, such as it is, is merely a
vehicle for satirical comment of the most varied kind on all
sorts of things, touching sometimes human nature in general,
sometimes the particular circumstances of the day and the
personalities of contemporaries. The licence of language
current at the time was very great, and Rabelais availed
himself of it to the fullest extent, partly because it suited his
humour, partly because it was dangerous to appear to take

things too earnestly. Nor is it true that his book is a satire with a definite purpose, such for instance as Swift's *Gulliver*. It is rather the outcome of an extraordinarily active and powerful brain, well stored with learning, assisted by an inexhaustible fancy, and not devoid of a certain moral sense. There is, for instance, no doubt that Rabelais had an original and remarkable theory of education, and that he was violently opposed to the abuses of the Church of Rome. But he was neither a Protestant nor an infidel, though attempts have been made to claim him for both parties. A very different book is the *Institution* of Calvin, which contains, so to speak, the constitution and code of all those religious bodies which at the Reformation definitely broke with Catholic tradition and declined to recognise the continuity of the Christian Church. Originally written in Latin, it was almost at once translated by its author, who saw the necessity of appealing to the people and not merely to the learned, and who indeed is responsible for the strong democratic feeling which accompanied the religious revolt in many cases. The style is entirely unlike anything that had before been known in French, being grave, sustained, and at the same time polished, and equally remote from the simple and inartistic phrase of the earlier chroniclers and from the heavy sentences, charged with foreign terms and constructions, which the first imitators of the classics had brought into fashion. The style of Calvin is on the face of it as much opposed to that of Rabelais as his substance. Yet the author of *Gargantua*, as if to show what in other circumstances he could have done, occasionally drops the fantastic mantle of exaggeration and burlesque in which he wraps himself, and then his language has an incomparable dignity and a sober grace superior to that of Calvin himself.

The immediate followers of Calvin were not remarkable

for literary proficiency. They imitated their master's scholarly
and classical style as best they could, but the result was
generally heavy and pedantic, so that *style refugié* became a
term of reproach. On the other hand, the example and the
enormous popularity of Rabelais also brought about a great
number of imitations. Some of these, as was natural, copied
only the worst parts of the master, and reproduced and
exaggerated his ribaldry and his extravagance, without aiming
at or caring for the fancy, the wit, and the occasional dignity
of thought to which that extravagance and that ribaldry were
for the most part little more than a cloak. The court of
Marguerite of Navarre produced, however, two volumes of
short tales in which the influence of Rabelais is less strong
perhaps than that of the earlier French tale and of Italian literature, but which are masterpieces of their kind. The first, the
Heptameron, is attributed to Marguerite herself. It is composed on the model of Boccaccio's *Decameron*, and the stories
of which it consists are supposed to be told on seven days
and a part of an eighth, by a company of noble guests
stopped by a flood on their way back from Cauterets in the
Pyrenees, then as now a fashionable watering-place. The
tales of the *Heptameron* have much intrinsic merit and charm,
and are besides highly characteristic of the polished society
of the time, which was a kind of aftermath of chivalry, with
more refined manners and greater intellectual development,
especially on the side of art-culture, but of somewhat more
corrupt morals. The Queen has left other works, genuine
or attributed, including some poems entitled *Les Marguerites
de la Marguerite*, but a strong suspicion is entertained that
she was not the author of the entire *Heptameron*, perhaps not
even of a large part of it. There were many of her literary
courtiers and favourites whose part authorship in it may
be guessed, notably Bonaventure des Périers (1500?–

1544 ?), who has left a short volume of acknowledged tales, *Contes et joyeux Devis*, not dissimilar in character though less elaborate. Des Périers was a free-thinker, and wrote a singular series of dialogues entitled *Cymbalum Mundi*, composed on the model of those of Lucian and not at all orthodox in tendency. It is believed that he committed suicide in consequence of the persecution which this work brought upon him, and from which the protection of Marguerite was an insufficient shield. Other writers of a somewhat similar kind were Jean Bouchet, Noel du Fail, the Seigneur de Cholières, and somewhat later Béroalde de Verville, the most Rabelaisian, in the good as well as the bad sense, of all. Perhaps also the well-known scholar Henri Estienne (1528–1598) should be classed with this group, in virtue of his curious *Apologie pour Hérodote*, a book nominally in defence of Herodotus, but really consisting of an attack on the Roman Catholic clergy, and indebted both to Rabelais and to the *Heptameron* for style and substance. The *Apologie* is an amusing book, and full of information about contemporary and earlier manners, but as literature it is far inferior to its models.

Another very important branch of the literature of the sixteenth century in France was history and memoir-writing, for the latter of which the French had already amply shown their capacity. Towards the end of the fifteenth century it became usual to write not merely chronicles of the writer's own time and experiences, with introductory summaries of other men's work, but also regular histories, either general or of France in particular. Such were written in our present period by Du Haillan, La Popelinière, and others, not without some glimmerings of the critical spirit. But the memoirs in which those who were actors or spectators of public affairs wrote down their own experience are far the most important branch of the historical writing of this time, both for the information they convey and for their literary merits. The memoirs of Blaise de Montluc (1503–1577), a soldier of fortune who distinguished himself in the Italian and religious wars, and was famous for the ruthless severity with which he enforced the royal authority against Catholic and Huguenot alike; of his brother marshals Vieilleville and Tavannes, the former written by his secretary, the latter by his son; of François de Lanoue (1531–1591), the distinguished Huguenot chieftain and one of the most moderate and esteemed politicians of the time, are the chief of these memoirs of the purely or mainly military kind. Marguerite de Valois (1553–1615), the first wife of Henri IV, has left memoirs which are very well written and extremely interesting. Pierre de l'Estoile (1546–1611) kept elaborate records of the events which came under his notice officially and unofficially. But the most famous memoirs of the whole century, memoirs which form one of the capital books of French literature, are those of Pierre de Bourdeilles, Abbé de Brantôme (1540–1614). Brantôme lived much about the court, and was an indefatigable collector of gossip of all sorts, which he has recorded without the slightest scruple. The form which his works take is a singular one. They consist of collections of brief biographies of the famous men and women of the time, under the head of *Vies des grands Capitaines, des Dames galantes*, &c. But there is very little method about them, and the author digresses continually. Nevertheless, though they have few pretensions to the observance of any literary rule, the vivacity, the truth of colouring, and the power of drawing character and relating anecdote which they display, are exceedingly great.

Towards the end of the century many prose works of remarkable excellence were written, besides those already mentioned, and of many different kinds. The *Satyre Ménippée*, a remarkable production, due to five or six different authors, was the first example of political satire conceived on the great scale and rewarded by great success. It helped the cause of Henri IV against the League not a little; and one of the sections which it contains, the discourse of Claude d'Aubray, the leader of the Tiers état, is an admirable piece of serious political writing, and like the whole work, one of the earliest of its kind. Half politicians, half lawyers, were Bodin (1530–1596), and Du Vair (1556–1621), the former a defender on philosophical principles of absolute government, the latter a constitutionalist of a moderate kind. A third lawyer who did not confine himself to his profession, but busied himself with literature, history, and antiquarianism generally, was Etienne Pasquier (1529–1615), whose *Recherches de la France* unite literary elegance, sound critical spirit, and great learning. What may be called scientific writing in the vulgar tongue was also practised at this time. Ambrose Paré, the great surgeon, was a good prose writer; Bernard Palissy, the potter, has left writings of value and interest; while Olivier de Serres set the example of treating economic subjects. Of a very different kind, but still more widely popular, and of great influence upon style, was the translation of *Amadis of Gaul*, which Herberay des Essarts undertook. France had so many romances of chivalry of her own that it may seem strange that she should go to Spain for another. *Amadis*, however, in Herberay's well-written version, became highly popular and was widely read. It is even said to have been the most usual reading book for foreigners learning the French language. Another translator takes rank among the very best prose writers of the time, and has always been a favourite study of Frenchmen who wished to write a pure and at the same time a picturesque and racy style. This was Jacques Amyot, bishop of Auxerre (1513–1593).

Translation from the classics was naturally practised to a very considerable extent at a time when the classics were regarded with so much interest and veneration. But no translator even approached the success of Amyot. His two chief works are his version of *Plutarch* and that of the *Daphnis and Chloe* of Longus. The former suited the taste of the time for stirring business and at the same time for moral reflection, and had a very great influence—an influence extended to England by imitations of it in our tongue. The *Daphnis and Chloe* hit equally well the peculiar feature of the day which we have alluded to in characterising the *Heptameron*. It is an exceedingly beautiful piece of prose, doing full justice to the exquisite pastoral it translates, in a language which, unlike the Greek of Longus, is in the height of its youthful vigour.

The coarse but forcible eloquence of the preachers of the preceding period was, in the third quarter of the century, revived in the midst of the excitement of the League. This revolutionary movement was directed at least as much against the house of Valois as against Protestantism, and the invectives of the preachers against Henri III and Henri IV were about equal in their virulence. The chief pulpit orators of the time were Boucher, Launay, and Guincestre, many of whose furious harangues have been preserved. They would hardly deserve the name of literature, were it not that they afford evidence of the enrichment of the language, and of the greater control which speakers and writers alike had gained over it for almost all purposes.

The most celebrated, and, from a literary point of view, beyond all question the greatest book, of the last half of the century, remains to be noticed. This is the *Essais* of Michel de Montaigne (1533–1592). Montaigne was a Gascon gentleman of the neighbourhood of Bordeaux, where his forefathers had long occupied a distinguished position in town and country. His family name was Eyquem, and it used to be thought that it was English by origin, but later research has made this doubtful. At any rate, he is the only French writer, except Rabelais, before our own day, who deserves in the English sense the name of humourist. His essays are very original in form, nor is there any previous author to whom he can be shown to have been indebted for the idea of them. Although full of anecdote, they are not narrative in the main, and start from some idea which has occurred to the author, some passage he has met in his reading, and the like. On this Montaigne comments, and allows his comment to lead him in any direction, without troubling himself at all about the text. According to the fashion of the time, he makes a considerable parade of learning and quotation, but no one can say that the quotations are the attraction of the book. The author, without possessing a highly poetical imagination, or much feeling of the deeper kind, has an incomparable common sense, a wide knowledge of life and human nature, great humour, and above all the peculiar faculty of saying anything that occurs to him without caring for the good or bad effect it may produce on the reader. His motto *Que sais-je?* only partially expresses him, for the presence of doubt is not so much the characteristic of Montaigne as the absence of dogmatism. As in the case of Rabelais, there is little ground for putting him down as a religious sceptic, though he certainly could not be called a devout member of any church. His attitude in politics is similar to his attitude in religion. The purely literary merits of Montaigne are very great. Without affecting the pedantry of the Pléiade, he did not scruple to use classical words whenever he was at a loss for a phrase to express his meaning. His sentences at the same time observe no regular rule of shortness or length, but are always clear and intelligible. Montaigne had an imitator of his peculiar style of sceptical moralising in Pierre Charron (1541–1603), who wrote a book entitled *De la Sagesse*. Neither in literary nor in philosophical merit however does this work even approach the *Essays*, which will always hold a foremost place among the triumphs of French literature.

CHAPTER V.

THE BEGINNING OF THE CLASSICAL PERIOD.

THE great writers who together represent the influence of the Renaissance in French literature, and of whom account has been given in the preceding chapter, contributed in point of intrinsic worth as important a mass of work as that supplied by the writers of any other period in French history. But partly from the circumstances of the time, partly perhaps from the very superabundance of their individual genius, they did not help to produce any one marked effect upon literature; each went his own way, save in the case of the Pléiade group, and even in their case more than might at first be supposed. Verse to some degree, and prose almost entirely, were written either according to the bent of the writer's individual taste and the character of his studies, or else in imitation of some particular author whom he set before him. The outcome of this was much admirable work; but no definite and uniform style, especially no definite and uniform prose style, resulted from it. The consequence is, that while the best sixteenth-century writers are exceedingly good, the ordinary run are perhaps not so good as they might be. A wide study of antiquity, and an extensive importation of foreign words and ideas, had moreover left the language in a somewhat chaotic state, and it so happened that at the end of the sixteenth and the beginning of the seventeenth century there were but few writers (perhaps only one) of the first genius for original composition. It was therefore not unnatural that the period should be one rather of criticism than of original performance. And though the criticism was in some cases unfortunate, it was in a great degree justified by the brilliant period of creation which followed.

At the time of which we are speaking—the end of the sixteenth century—the mediæval influence, properly so-called, was entirely exhausted, and no trace remains of it as an active and living force. The surest sign of this is, that people now began to imitate mediæval work—as in the case of the famous *Vaux de Vire*, written by Jean le Houx, a Norman lawyer, and attributed to Olivier Basselin—and even to edit and study it as a purely literary and antiquarian task. The school of Marot had left no very definite successors, and that of the Pléiade had worn itself out, partly owing to its undue pedantry, partly to the error, constantly recurring in the history of literature, which had induced its members to form themselves into a kind of sect or clique. At the same time the first energy of the Renaissance, and the enjoyment and delight in living and learning which had characterised it, had died out in the midst of the terrible wars of the League period. The great range of modern science, and the necessity of attaching oneself more or less definitely to some particular branch of it, also began to be recognised, at the same time that the critical spirit began to make its first mark on literature. These two influences, the spirit of subdivision and the critical spirit, preside over all the work of the seventeenth century, and are responsible both for its merits and its defects.

In poetry proper the result of these new influences did not produce any work of the very first class after the first years of the century. Desportes and Bertaut, the last of the school of Ronsard, were not strong men. Mathurin Regnier

(1573–1613), the nephew of Desportes, was indeed a great poet, with a strong and flexible versification and vocabulary, and an almost equal command over the tender and the satirical style in poetry. His satires, with those of D'Aubigné, are perhaps the best that French literature has produced, while some of his minor poems are full of pathos. But Regnier occupied a somewhat isolated position, and exercised but little influence. The poet of the time was François de Malherbe (1556–1628), a poor enough writer as far as real poetical merits go, but one who had the luck or the merit to recognise the taste of the day, and to meet or rather to anticipate it. Malherbe set himself to oppose the classical tendencies of the Pléiade by substituting for them other aims of a not dissimilar kind. He it was who set the example of the characteristics which distinguished French poetry for fully two centuries, and which made it the admiration of all Europe, while at the same time they now make it in parts very difficult to read. These characteristics may be thus summed up,—a very accurate versification and manner of rhyming, the use exclusively of a carefully chosen and conventional phraseology, the avoidance of picturesque or startling language and effects, and the preference of a kind of elegant commonplace in the treatment of every subject.

The principles of Malherbe did not at once take root in French poetry, yet there was no poet sufficiently strong to resist their gradual introduction, though Regnier did what he could. The first half of the seventeenth century produced indeed many rhymers of talent, but after Regnier's death no poet of genius, in France. The two chiefs of Malherbe's direct disciples, Racan (1589–1670) and Maynard (1582–1646), were correct and elegant versifiers; especially the first, who may be said to have had not a few sparks of the true poetic fire. Side by side with these, and somewhat later, there existed three different schools of poetry, while a singular and unequal poet, Théophile de Viaud, occupies a position by himself. These three schools, in the order of time, and perhaps of literary importance, were the school of writers of *vers de société*, that of Bacchanalian poets, and that of the producers of ponderous epics. Of the first the chief supporter was Voiture (1598-1648), to whose name may be joined those of Benserade, Sarrasin, Segrais and Charleval. Saint-Amant (1594-1660), a vigorous writer, was the chief representative of the second; and the third had at its head the much-ridiculed Chapelain (1595-1674), author of the *Pucelle*, and included besides a priest of some talent, the Père Lemoine (1602-1671), members who busied themselves also with other poetic forms, such as the just-mentioned Saint-Amant and Georges de Scudéry (1601-1667).

While the purism of Malherbe was slowly making its way in French verse, a similar and much more healthy influence was being exerted in the department of prose by Jean Guez de Balzac (1594-1654)—the elder Balzac, as he is often called to distinguish him from the great novelist of the nineteenth century. Balzac was a man of family and position, who seems to have had very little to write about, but who, perhaps for that reason, was extremely careful about his manner of writing. In his letters, essays, and a moral treatise called the *Socrate Chrétien*, he endeavoured to purify the vocabulary and regulate the style of ordinary prose writing, which hitherto had been, except in the hands of a few great writers, by no means a convenient instrument for general literary purposes. These various reforming influences were largely assisted by the formation of the Academy, and by the fancy of the time for literary coteries, in which authors and ladies of rank played the chief parts, but which were also frequented by many statesmen and nobles. The famous Madame de Rambouillet was the chief patroness of these meetings, at which much minor poëtry and many short prose pieces were composed or recited. Connected more or less intimately with these meetings were the ponderous prose romances which are generally associated with the period in literary memory. The popularity of the *Amadis* has been mentioned. But since the *Amadis* had been translated, not merely the fashion of writing but the fashion of thinking had changed a good deal, and something different from mere tales of fighting and enchantment was required. Accordingly, writers like Gomberville, La Calprenède, Mademoiselle de Scudéry, wrote *Cléopâtre, Le grand Cyrus, Clélie*, and many other works, in which formal gallantry and love-casuistry, with noble sentiments of various kinds, were illustrated at immense length. Influences too many to be here discussed were at work on these curious and now forgotten compositions. But the principal native forerunner of them was a singular work, the *Astrée* of Honoré d'Urfé (1567-1623). This, which bears some faint resemblance to our *Arcadia*, represents a kind of pastoral society on the banks of the Lignon, a river traversing the writer's own estates in the south of France. Of a much more genuine kind in the department of prose fiction were the burlesques of Scarron (1610-1660), the chief of which is the *Roman Comique*, an interesting sketch of the life of strolling actors in the provinces, and the extravaganzas of Cyrano de Bergerac (1620-1655). The last writer, who was a dramatist as well, composed a *Voyage au Soleil* and *Voyage à la Lune*, in which the influence of Rabelais is evident.

The really great developments of French literature in this first half of the century, while Louis XIII was on the throne, or during the minority of his son, were of a very different kind. During the sixteenth century, abundant as had been the exercise given to the intellect, that exercise had, in the most

serious and abstract subjects, been chiefly confined to religious
disputes on questions of church government and a few
points of dogma. The unseemly controversies of the earlier
religious struggles, and the furious preachings of the League,
were succeeded by religious polemics of a more decent kind,
and by pulpit eloquence which promised the great oratorical
displays of the latter part of the century. The chief partakers in this were, on the Protestant side, Duplessis-Mornay
(1549–1623), a scholarly and forcible writer; on the side of
Rome, the Cardinal du Perron (1555–1618), a great master
of argument, and Saint Francis of Sales (1567–1622), famous
as a preacher and a writer of devout meditations as well as
for his polemical writings. But the thought of the new age
threw itself still more into purely philosophical lines, and into
subjects which appeared less dangerous to handle. The old
scholastic philosophy, which, in various shapes, had sufficed
the philosophical appetite of the middle ages, had been
practically dead for a long time, though its forms still
continued to be taught in colleges and universities. The
sixteenth century, in this as in other things showing its
reverence for classical antiquity, had tried, but without
success, to satisfy itself with the actual text of the Greek
philosophers. It is the glory of France to have produced, in
René Descartes (1596–1650), at once one of the earliest and
most skilful writers of a clear, elegant, and scholarly prose in
any modern language, and also the first great modern philosopher, taking philosophy in its strictest meaning. The
Discours de la Méthode and the *Méditations* of Descartes treat
of the most abstruse subjects that can possibly occupy human
thought, yet they are written in French so clear and simple
that any child, as far as the mere literal and grammatical
meaning goes, can understand them at once. Nor did the
spirit of discussion stop at profane philosophy. Many points

of Christian theology, which had not been made the subject of the great half political, half ecclesiastical disputes of the sixteenth century, came in for discussion and study. Among these, the questions of freewill, etc., were handled by a Dutch theologian named Jansenius (1583–1638), and from him a school or sect of religious thinkers, who had themselves no inclination to separate from the Church of Rome, and no suspicion that their tenets involved any disloyalty to her, grew up in France. From the first this school was of great literary and philosophical importance; it adopted ardently much of the philosophy of Descartes, published an important work on logic (called, from the chief home of the school, the Port Royal Logic), and in Arnauld, Nicole, and others, produced men of letters of great eminence. It produced also, after a time, one of the greatest of all French writers, a man superior even to Descartes from the purely literary point of view, Blaise Pascal (1623–1662), the author of the *Pensées* and of the letters called for shortness the *Provinciales*. These latter, which are among the masterpieces of the literature of the world, were drawn forth by a dispute that had arisen between the Jansenists and Jesuits, a dispute which in the long run was fatal to the former. But, so far as Pascal's book is concerned, the victory rested wholly with him, and it may be said that in more than two centuries the Jesuits have never got over it. All the faults and absurdities that could be found in the principles or practice of that famous order are exposed in the *Provinciales* with the most exquisite literary skill, and with irony which for the first time was completely presented in literature. There is, at least in the earlier letters, no direct attack or harsh language, but the persons and theories attacked are steeped in such a bath of ridicule, held up to such unpitying derision, that to this day the book serves as a pattern and a storehouse to everybody who wishes to perfect himself in the art of polite attack. Pascal's other great work is of a different kind. No other *Pensées* have more depth or greater range than Pascal's, but in what is technically called 'form,' that is to say in perfection of style and literary arrangement, they are inferior for the most part to the *Provinciales.* This is due to their being rather rough notes, intended for subsequent working up, than finished productions.

The renown which France had already acquired for memoir-writing did not decline in this age, from which many famous books of the kind date, and which supplied in its turbulent and changeable politics abundance of materials for the purpose. Conspicuous among such writers is the great Cardinal of Richelieu, who ·though not exactly the founder of the Academy, as he is sometimes ignorantly called, brought it for the first time into a solid and stable condition, and transformed it from a mere private club of wits, such as the century saw many, into an institution formally charged with the overseeing of French language and literature. It has already been observed that the time was very propitious for such an institution, owing to the habits of criticism which Malherbe and Balzac had introduced. There was also all the more reason for it that what may be called the profession of literature was, for the first time, assuming a regular position. In the middle ages men who wrote were either persons of distinction writing for their own pleasure, or else for the most part dependents upon such persons writing to please their patrons and masters. The printing press, and the growth of education and of a desire for knowledge, if they had not made writing certainly and absolutely profitable, had at any rate connected with it the possibilities of profit. It so happened, too, that at this time a form of literature which had been long pursued rose greatly in the public estimation, and offered something like a regular livelihood to those who could hit the public taste. This was the drama, with which some of the greatest triumphs of French literature in the seventeenth century are indissolubly associated, and of the state of which some account must now be given, as account has already been given of the mediæval theatre in France.

Towards the middle of the sixteenth century a great alteration took place by the prohibition, at least in Paris, of the acting of miracle-plays and mysteries. The Confraternity of the Passion, when their licence was renewed, were expressly confined to profane dramas, though mysteries continued to be acted for some considerable time in the provinces. The profane mystery however held its ground, as also did the morality, while the farce was more popular than ever. But the establishment of the form of French drama which was to gain most celebrity and popularity was, as has been noticed in passing, a work, and the most durable work, of the Pléiade. The tragedies which Jodelle imitated were not so much those of the great masters of Greek drama as the singular pieces, sometimes full of merit, sometimes quite devoid of it, which have come down to us under the name of Seneca. There was something in these plays, their regular arrangement, their stately declamation, and the somewhat stilted grandeur of their sentiments, which commended itself peculiarly to the French mind. Besides the classical subjects, which could be copied more or less directly from Seneca, the Bible (which, it must be remembered, was a novel possession in the vulgar tongue at this time, and perhaps the most popular of all books wherever it was permitted to be read) furnished numerous stirring themes. Jodelle's example was followed by Grévin, De la Taille, and many others. Shortly, too, there arose a dramatist of great talent to help the popularity of the model. This was Robert Garnier (1545–1601), whose faculty of versification was praised by Ronsard, and whose chief plays (*Les Juives*, a tragedy on the fall of Jerusalem under Nebuchadnezzar; *Bradamante*, a tragi-comedy from Ariosto; *Cornélie*, a classical piece) have great merit both as poetry and as drama. In these pieces the chorus, as in the classical drama, plays a very important part, and some of the finest passages of Garnier's work are to be found in these choruses, for which the French of the sixteenth century was well suited. Garnier was followed by Antoine de Montchrestien (d. 1621), a Huguenot, who lived a stormy life at the end of the sixteenth and the beginning of the seventeenth century. Montchrestien wrote several plays, including one on the contemporary sufferings of Mary Queen of Scots, which was probably the first of the many dramas devoted to that ill-fated queen, and one on the story of Haman and Mordecai, from which Racine afterwards borrowed something. Montchrestien's choruses (for choruses still continued to be used) are often very fine. It ought to be observed that these plays are in the main of entirely the same character as those which afterwards made French drama famous, and that the idea of Corneille and Racine having invented this drama, or of their having borrowed it from the heroic romances of the Scudéry type (a strange fancy which has often been repeated) is wholly erroneous. There was however in them what we should call a great deficiency of practical acting merit. The speeches are far too long, there is rarely any action, and what there is is interrupted by the chorus and its performances. The father of the French stage, as far as the function of the playwright proper is concerned, was Alexandre Hardy (1560–1631). Hardy was regularly engaged by a troop of actors, one of many which existed at this time both as strollers about the country and as stationary in the large towns, and he produced an enormous number of plays, in many of which he was indebted to Spanish originals. Writing as Hardy did, directly for representation, and under the eyes, so to speak, of the actors, he was certain to consult acting capabilities and popular taste almost before anything else. His plays, while sometimes containing passages of no little merit, are rather intended to be acted than to be read. They have plenty of action, of lively dialogue, and of striking situations, but often sin in the direction of bombast and rant. It was significant too of the taste of the time that Hardy never (though another playwright, Jean de Schélandre, nearly did so) ventured on the complex action and free development of the English play. Something like the classical standard of unities was always maintained. At the beginning of the seventeenth century there were a large number of dramatists, none of them of much merit ; but by the termination of the first quarter of it, things began to improve. Mairet, Du Ryer, Tristan, wrote plays of some pretension both for acting capacity and literary merit. Rotrou (1609–1650), the immediate predecessor of Corneille, next appeared. Rotrou's best work (*Venceslas, St. Genest*) was not produced until Corneille had set him the example. Pierre Corneille himself (1606–1684), the first French dramatist of the highest class, and perhaps, as far as tragedy goes, the only dramatist of that class which France has produced, did not begin with a masterpiece. His first play, *Mélite*, a lively bustling comedy, is only a little better than contemporary work ; and his second, *Clitandre*, a preposterous tragedy of the school of Hardy, is only a little more absurd than its rivals. Like Balzac the novelist, Corneille did a great deal of work before doing anything decidedly good or characteristic. At length *Médée*, a fine tragedy on a fine subject, 'announced Corneille' as has been happily said, and the announcement was soon fulfilled by the appearance of the *Cid*. A desperate critical controversy sprung up about this famous play. Corneille's patron, Richelieu, was to a certain extent jealous of him, and the then new Academy was set to criticise the work, while envious rivals, such as Claveret and Mairet, did their best to write it down. It was all in vain. 'All Paris,' as the stock quotation has it, 'had for Chimène the eyes of Rodrigue,' and it gained at once the popularity it has never lost with lovers of magnanimous passion and full-toned verse. Its author's great qualities were further shown, and his fame conclusively established, by *Cinna* and *Horace*. Unfortunately for himself, Corneille outlived his popularity though not his genius; and his last works, which belong to the next period, were contrasted with the weaker but fresher, and, to the taste of the time, more attractive dramas of Racine. But the plays already mentioned, with *Rodogune* and *Polyeucte* (perhaps his two best works), were all produced comparatively early. Corneille's chief characteristics are the stateliness and grandeur of his thought and of the verse in which he dresses it. His range is not very wide, nor is he particularly happy in the delineation of ordinary character or of the softer and lighter feelings ; yet he managed, with some help from a Spanish original, to write the best comedy, *Le Menteur*, before Molière. The display of heroic sentiments and conduct, such as Rodrigue's sacrifice of love to honour and filial affection, Horace's elevation of the idea of patriotism above all domestic ties, Polyeucte's religious zeal setting at nought the chance or rather certainty of losing his private happiness, are the subjects which Corneille can perfectly treat. His most famous single piece of verse, the splendid declamation of Camille when she learns that her brother has slain her lover, is perhaps unapproached in its kind, or only approached by other pieces of the same author. But Corneille, like every French dramatist, fails when he is compared with our own great playwriters, by reason of the partial and exaggerated view which he gives of human nature, and of his inability to depict the more individual kinds of character. It is probable that these drawbacks are due at least as much to the form of play which, by his time, was the accepted and almost the only possible one in France, as to his own shortcomings. The ideas of regularity and correctness which had been strongly impressed on French literature, even before his birth, were by this time thoroughly established, and his audience would have been shocked at the free display of action, the complicated, story, the abundant characters, which allowed Shakespeare and his great followers to show at once their knowledge of human nature and the resources of their literary art.

CHAPTER VI.

THE age of Louis XIV in French literature is one of the numerous periods of history which have had to pay the penalty of exaggerated and uncritical admiration. It produced only one of the very greatest names, Molière; and three of such names, those of Corneille, Descartes, and Pascal, which are sometimes borrowed to increase its lustre, belong undoubtedly to an earlier time. In the highest branch of letters, poetry pure and simple, it was sterile. The critical principles which were chiefly professed, if not solely observed in it, led to the impoverishment and degradation of the language and its literature. But when deduction has been made for all these things, it has still to be confessed that but few periods, not merely of French history but of any other, can vie with it in the production of work of permanent value. With Molière to represent the class of names of which the whole world cannot furnish more than a score or so ; with La Fontaine, Racine, La Rochefoucauld, Malebranche, Bossuet, Fénelon, to be classed among those who only just miss this highest honour; with Saint-Evremond, Boileau, La Bruyère, Madame de Sevigné, Saint-Simon, Massillon, Bourdaloue, Hamilton, Perrault, Regnard, Quinault, St. Réal, and many more holding hardly a lower place as regards their best work,—the time must always have a great claim on the attention of literary students, and the shortsightedness and narrowness of its prevailing literary principles must be pardoned in favour of the excellence of its general literary practice.

The most prominent place in the literature of the age of Louis XIV is usually assigned to the drama, of which Molière and Racine were the great representatives, Corneille, though he was actually their contemporary, and continued to write almost as long as either, belonging clearly to an elder generation in character as well as in age. For perfection in his own style Molière (1622–1673) is undoubtedly the greatest of all comic writers. In verbal wit he is not quite the equal of Congreve, but his wit is used with much better taste, and is allied with a far deeper and wider conception of human nature. In giving comedy a poetical aspect, and in taking in all the intricacies of character, he is the inferior of Shakespeare. In rich humour he certainly yields to Aristophanes, and in dry humour possibly to Plautus. But for orderly and regular treatment of his themes, with reference at once to literary standards to the truth of nature and to the requirements of the stage, he has never been, and is never likely to be surpassed. His two greatest plays, *Tartuffe*, a satire on religious hypocrisy, and *Le Misanthrope*, a satire on the frivolity of fashionable life, are almost impossible to be excelled; and it may be said of Molière that he is the one great dramatist who has persistently kept before his eyes the moral purpose which is always asserted to be one of the chief merits of the stage. The only charge that can fairly be brought against his plays is that, notwithstanding the range of their subjects and the truth of their handling, each one is apt to take too limited a view of the characters with which it deals. To explain what is meant we may compare Molière with the master of all literature. When Shakespeare draws Falstaff, he does not make him a mere type of cowardice or of sensual indulgence. He gives strokes that show how in other circumstances the fat knight might have been, and probably was, a brave and honourable man. The soul of goodness in things evil, and contrariwise the weakness and 'dram of eale' in things good, is never forgotten by him. Even Iago is rather warped by a devilish special purpose than wholly diabolical. Tartuffe, on the contrary, is little more than embodied hypocrisy, and Alceste little more than embodied pride and impatience of that with which he does not sympathise. This tendency to produce types rather than individuals had been characteristic of French literature in very early times, had broken out conspicuously in the allegorical school of poetry which reigned for two centuries, and was strongly assisted at the time we are discussing by the adoption of the artificial rules of the 'unities' which the critics forced upon the poets. It is clearly difficult, if not impossible, to show the natural complexity of human characters on a stage where the action is strictly limited to the display of a definite and particular plot, where little or nothing is allowed to be done as well as spoken, where the story has to pass in a few hours, and even the scene is scarcely changed. These rigorous restrictions were not indeed enforced in comedy to the same extent as in tragedy; and the former was consequently able to develop itself much better than the latter. But still there was a general tendency in the same direction, and one of the signs of it may be found in the fancy for entitling plays (*Le Misanthrope, Le Joueur*, &c.) so as to show beforehand that one aspect of character was intended to be kept in view. The notion of the ruling passion may be said to be at the bottom of French comedy, if not as Molière wrote it, at any rate as his successors, the greatest of whom was Regnard, adopted it from him.

In tragedy the matter was much worse. It became by degrees understood that the persons of tragedy must do nothing but talk, and in the tragedy of Racine (1639–1699) and his successors they do nothing else. Now there are but few situations endless talk about which can be made interesting to audiences and readers. The chief of these few situations is what is called making love, and Racine, submitting himself to the critical ideas of the time, adopted this situation as the only one in most of his plays (*Phèdre, Iphigénie, Mithridate,* &c.). *Athalie* and *Esther* are to be excepted, and, curiously enough, they contain his best work. The author, it is true, shows extraordinary talent in handling his limited theme, and he has so exactly hit the taste and ideas of his countrymen that even now, when the critical unsoundness of the ideas under which he wrote has long been demonstrated, his plays continue to be frequently acted with applause, and sometimes read with pleasure. It was also much in Racine's favour that he was one of the most industrious and careful of writers, and was possessed of an extraordinarily equable talent. His great rival, Corneille, though far his superior both as a poet and a dramatist, was a rapid and a very unequal writer. Between the passages which to the present day strike both eye and ear with the crash of thunder and the brilliance of lightning, there are long tracts of the most dreary monotony and insignificance in Corneille. Racine, on the other hand, by his marvellous attention to his language and versification, maintains a pretty uniform level of attractiveness. With Pope and Virgil he is perhaps the greatest of all poets whose claim to immortality is that they have thoroughly mastered the formal part of poetry. The value of these, though at times it may be overrated and at times underrated, is permanent and cannot be destroyed. But in Racine's contemporaries and successors, such as Campistron (1656–1737), Pradon (1632–1698), Duché (1668–1704), La Fosse (1653–1708), the faults of whose plan and material are as great or greater, while their merits are far inferior, the result is nearly intolerable, and between Racine and Voltaire there are few French tragedies, except the works of the elder Crébillon (1674-1763), which deserve to be read or even mentioned.

The critical opinions which these poets obeyed were not—indeed prevailing critical opinions never are—the opinions of any one person. They had been started by the admiration of antiquity affected by the Pléiade, formulated in a manner very disastrous to their originators by Malherbe, continued by the chief constituents of the early Academy. But they were finally laid down as laws by the most famous of all French critics, Nicholas Boileau Despréaux (1636–1711). This celebrated man had a keen but narrow intellect, a fair knowledge of the Latin classics, some considerable skill in handling and teaching others to handle one form of French verse, little acquaintance with Greek, no taste whatever for the higher poetry, and a complete ignorance of the earlier literature of his own and the contemporary literature of other countries. He thus lacked what is perhaps the very first requisite of poetical criticism, a wide acquaintance with poetry in different tongues, to prevent the critic from · mistaking its accidental for its essential elements. He did a great deal to narrow and weaken French poetical literature, though he did something also to give formal perfection to those branches of it which his taste admitted. His rude ridicule did service by putting an end to the ponderous epics of the Chapelain school and the extravagances of some of the earlier tragedians; but except as regards the structure of the Alexandrine, that is to say of one kind of Alexandrine, he had little positive value. He could only decry, and his talents in this direction were constantly misused, as in the case of Quinault (1635–1688) and Brébeuf (1618–1661), poets of limited merit, but, as poets, far superior to himself. He did not, however, confine himself to criticism: his satires, chiefly borrowed from Horace, are fairly good; and his burlesque poem of the *Lutrin*, in which he was also indebted, though in a less degree, to others, has merit. But his higher flights, such as his ode on the taking of Namur, are ridiculous compounds of bombast and platitude, and show that the man who could publish them must have been entirely blind to the requisites of true poetry For it is never to be forgotten that, though no one can call upon the critic to write good verse, he may fairly be called upon not to write verse that is bad.

A better critical spirit than Boileau's was represented by Saint-Evremond (1613–1703), who also deserves a considerable place as a literary moralist. The great fame and success of Montaigne had made it fashionable to treat all sorts of subjects essay-fashion, and there was hardly any limit to these exercises, which were often pursued in the literary côteries already commented upon. At one time the fashion was for what were called 'conversations'—short narratives of real or imaginary interviews between people of more or less celebrity. At another time it was for literary studies on particular kinds of verse or prose; at another for what were called 'portraits,' that is to say elaborate sketches of character of the kind of which Clarendon's *History* contains so many in English; at another for *Pensées* or *Maxims*, which were detached reflections, the former of no great length, the latter drawn up in the shortest possible form of words. Saint-Evremond excelled in most of these, as well as in letter-writing. His *Conversation du Maréchal d'Hocquincourt avec le Père Canaye* is one of the liveliest and most lifelike of all such pictures of manners and thoughts; his

'Thoughts on French Tragedies,' and his 'Dissertation on the word *Vaste*,' are models of literary criticism, and his character of the Duke de Candale has never been surpassed. The *Pensée* and the *Maxim* he did not much practise. The former has been noticed in the last chapter. Of the latter, the Duke de la Rochefoucauld (1613–1680), a great noble who had taken a share in the Fronde, and who has left memoirs of an important kind, was the chief writer. La Rochefoucauld has never been excelled in the power of packing the greatest amount of meaning into the fewest and best chosen words. Most of his maxims are of the moral kind, and perhaps do not express a very elevated view of morality or of human nature. But La Rochefoucauld, much as he had mixed with his fellows, had almost always seen them in unfavourable lights, first in the anarchy of the Fronde, and secondly in the period of general seeking for court favour which followed the majority of Louis XIV. Personally he was regarded with great respect by almost all his contemporaries. This kind of sententious moral writing was at a rather later period taken up by a somewhat inferior writer, La Bruyère (1639–1696), who developed it chiefly in the form of imaginary characters suggested by those of Theophrastus. La Bruyère has been called inferior to La Rochefoucauld, but this relative inferiority does not imply any inferiority to writers in general. La Bruyère was a great master of French, French rather of the newer and more polished but weaker type that resulted from the criticism of Boileau, than of the vigorous elder language which, with an improvement in grace but no loss of energy, La Rochefoucauld was able to employ.

In somewhat close connection with this moralist literature stands that of history, memoirs, and letters, in which the age hardly yields to either of those that immediately preceded it.

To Louis XIV's reign belong the most famous letter-writer and the most famous memoir-writer of France, though the latter somewhat outlived in point of time the period to which his works properly belong in spirit as well as in subject. No writer of memoirs has ever approached the Duke de Saint-Simon (1675–1755) in vividness, originality, and irregular power. No writer of letters has ever approached Madame de Sévigné (1627–1697) in natural grace, in fulness of interest, and in power of attracting the reader to the personality of the writer. By the side of these distinguished names might be grouped a very long list of both descriptions of authors, among whom Madame de Maintenon (1635–1719) would hold a place not very far below Madame de Sévigné, Dangeau one a good deal below Saint-Simon, and Tallemant des Réaux, a writer of curious and scandalous anecdotes called *Historiettes*, one quite by itself.

Nor while the contributions which were being made to the materials of history were so numerous was regular history-making neglected. It is true that at this time the spirit of historical criticism was not felt, and that what is called the philosophy of history was not as yet dreamt of. But Mézeray's (1610–1683) History of France is really a great work, showing both historical insight and literary skill of the first class ; and a large number of other writers followed in his steps. Pellisson (1624–1693) was a very accomplished writer both of political and literary history. Less remarkable for style, but still of merit, is Péréfixe (1605-1670), while d'Orleans (1644–1698), Daniel (1649–1728), and Rapin, the refugee historian of England (1661–1725), also deserve mention. Moreover, among the numerous fancies of the age for amicable literary competition, history had its share. It was for a time fashionable to take short striking episodes and handle them in the polished and nervous language which the union of ancient vigour and modern correctness had placed at the disposal of the prose writer. Such, rather before our present period, were the Cardinal de Retz's *Conjuration de Fiesque*, and Sarrasin's *Waldstein* (Wallenstein), such, later (1672), the Abbé de Saint-Réal's *Conjuration de Venise*, three tracts which perhaps carry the art of historical narration on the small scale to as high a pitch as is from the literary point of view possible. In connection with the subject of history too must be mentioned the vast and precious labours of men who were purely scholars, and who availed themselves of the leisure which was given them, sometimes by the endowments of the Church and especially of the monasteries, sometimes by their own private fortune, or by the easy public appointments common under unreformed governments, to research and compile. In not a few cases the materials they worked up have since perished, even if the handling of them were not beyond the degenerate strength and patience of modern scholars. Such were Fleury (1640–1723), Tillemont (1637–1698), Ducange (1614–1688), Mabillon (1622–1707).

As in poetry proper, in which the labourers of the period were so insignificant that they hardly require mention here, so in prose fiction, the department of literature which with the prose drama comes nearest to poetry, its achievements were not great. They were however decidedly greater than its poetical performances, and deserve some notice. Indeed if we throw La Fontaine into this class (and his works are little more than easy rhymed prose), the department becomes one of the most important of all. The huge romances of the heroic class continued to be popular, but there was already a reaction against them. This produced on the one hand the now forgotten tales of Madame de Villedieu (1631–1683), and on the other what may be considered as the starting-point of the modern novel, the works of Madame de la Fayette (*La Prin-*

cesse de Clèves, Zaïde). ' Madame de la Fayette (1633–1693) was a great friend of La Rochefoucauld and of Madame de Sévigné; her novels are not remarkable for vigour, but have plenty of delicate character-drawing, and are perhaps the first which aim strictly at the delineation of actual and probable life and sentiment, without regard to the conventions of the romance. But the best fiction of the time in point of absolute literary goodness is to be found in short stories, and especially in the fairy tales, for which there was a great demand towards the close of the century. Such things have never been better done than in the works of Charles Perrault (1628–1703) and Anthony Hamilton (1640–1720), while those of Madame d'Aulnoy (d. 1705), though perhaps inferior in literary art, preserve very happily the simplicity and grace of the original myths. All these prose tale-tellers, however, fall far short of the literary eminence of the verse tale-teller La Fontaine (1621–1695), who ranks among the men of letters of the period above Racine, and only below Molière. La Fontaine was a man of curious personal character. Absent, indifferent, and generally childlike in tastes and sympathies, but possessed of a fine literary taste and a rare literary faculty, he ranks as a direct descendant of the old fabliau-writers, and may indeed be described as the best fabliau-writer the world has ever produced. His two great works are different in subject but not dissimilar in manner and merit. His *Contes* are for the most part taken from older prose and verse originals, and often deal with matters not exactly edifying; but the wonderful narrative grace, the sly humour of the comment, the ingenuity of the moral reflections, and the knowledge of human nature which, like Goldsmith (also a kind of baby and plaything to his intimates), La Fontaine possessed, appear in every page. The same qualities without the drawbacks also appear in the

Fables by which he is most known. This difficult kind of work, in which the writer has to be simple without being trivial, and wise without giving himself airs of wisdom, has never been so well done as by La Fontaine.

Perhaps in no period of history have preachers and theologians played such an important part, from the literary point of view, as in the age of Louis XIV. The inclination of the time to purely abstract speculation had not yet generally taken a freethinking turn, nor was it checked in handling questions of controversy by the presence of active religious conflicts. Until the close of the century the Protestants were quietly tolerated in France, and the quarrel between the Jansenists and Jesuits was only after a time carried out of the range of literature by the interference of the secular arm. The king's defence of the Gallican Church against Ultramontanism, too, communicated to theology in France the national spirit which has always been of more importance as a motive in that country than in almost any other. The greatest of all the sacred orators of modern times, Bossuet (1627–1704), stands at the head of the literary theologians of the day in France. Bossuet's general manner was of a grand and almost rough stateliness, holding strongly by the Biblical style, and indulging but little in the minor graces and elegances of language. Something of the same kind was characteristic of Bourdaloue (1632–1704), while Fléchier (1632–1710) and Mascaron (1634–1703) approach nearer to the model of sixteenth-century writers, and abound in learned citations and quaint ornaments of rhetoric. On the other side, the Protestants Claude (1617–1687) and Saurin (1677–1730) deserve notice in this connection. The most famous of pulpit orators next to Bossuet was of a somewhat younger generation. Massillon (1663–1742) preached his most brilliant sermon on the death of Louis XIV, and survived his subject full thirty years. His style was more elegant and persuasive than that of the authors already mentioned. Fénelon (1651–1715) has been postponed because his genius was less purely ecclesiastical and theological than that of the others. Bossuet indeed wrote a sketch of universal history, but it was entirely from the theological point of view. Fénelon's works were of a much more miscellaneous character. His famous romance of *Télemaque* has perhaps been read by more foreigners than any· other French book published during the last two centuries and a half, not excepting the tragedies of Racine or the fables of La Fontaine. His political wisdom was great, and his views on the state of France accurate and far-sighted. Almost alone of his contemporaries he regarded with dislike and suspicion the innovating and restrictive criticism which had begun with Malherbe and had cul- minated in Boileau. Though himself a most correct and elegant writer, according to the current standard of elegance and correctness, he regretted the rich vocabulary and daring attempts of the Pléiade, and prophesied that the result of the modern theory could only in the long run be poverty and constraint.

Last of the long array of subjects must be mentioned philosophy, proper and applied. The brilliant work of Descartes had made a durable impression on the century, and all the prominent thinkers were for a time Cartesians. The Cartesian philosophy was, it must be remembered, a highly idealist philosophy, and it thus lent itself almost equally to cultivation in connection with or in neglect of religion. The greatest of the religious philosophers (one of the greatest of all philosophers as far as the history of literature has to do with philosophy) was Malebranche (1631– 1715). His great work, the *Recherche de la Vérité*, is written in

one of the clearest and most beautiful of styles—so much so,
that notwithstanding its highly abstract character, and the
absence of any deliberate attempt to conciliate the reader by
ornament and illustration, it is delightful to read.   Clearness
and precision were indeed of the essence of the philosophy of
Descartes, but few writers succeed in associating with them
so great a literary charm as Malebranche.   On the sceptical
side, the greatest literary representative of philosophy was
Pierre Bayle (1647–1706), nominally a Cartesian in philosophy and a Protestant in religion, but really a sceptic on
almost all points of intellectual interest.   Bayle's chief work
is his *Dictionary*, which is not 'a lexicon but a kind of very
unmethodical encyclopædia, · giving an account of and discussing various controverted points, or points of general interest, in history, literature, philosophy, and religion.   It was
one of the earliest books of the kind, and had a very great
influence both from the amount of information it contained
and from the freshness and piquancy of its ironical doubt.
Regarded purely from the point of style, Bayle is not worthy
to be ranked with the best of the writers already mentioned,
but his importance in literary history is very great, because
he acted as teacher to a large number of writers who gave
tone and character to the next age in literature as well as in
philosophy.   The desultory character of his work is also
significant of the taste of the day for miscellaneous literary
undertakings.   The *littérateur* of all work was a creation of
the time, and a good example of this class was Thomas
Corneille (1625–1709), the younger brother of Pierre, who
was a voluminous play-writer, a journalist, a grammarian,
and an editor of gazetteers.

CHAPTER VII.

THE EIGHTEENTH CENTURY.

THE literature which is usually spoken of as the literature of the eighteenth century in France, does not in reality extend in point of time of composition over the whole of the hundred years between 1700 and 1800. It is confined to the reigns of Louis XV and Louis XVI; nor does its palmy time even cover the whole of this interval of seventy or eighty years. Like the last years of the reign of Louis XIV, the first years of that of his great grandson were very unfruitful in literature, and the Revolution did not at first produce much literary work of interest or of value. Until the third or fourth decade of the century was reached there are few names of mark except those of some long-lived survivors of the former age. So also, after the death of Voltaire and Rousseau in 1778 little of value was produced for many years. Thus the literary activity of the time, one of the most influential if not the most intrinsically valuable of all literary periods, may almost be limited to the manhood and old age of Voltaire.

There is a good deal more in this limitation than mere chronological coincidence. The eighteenth century in France is, from the literary point of view, more emphatically the age of Voltaire than any other literary period can be said to be the age of any single man. Not merely did François Marie Arouet, called Voltaire (1694–1778), actually attempt almost

every branch of literature with great success, but the spirit
which animated most if not all of his work was emphatically
the spirit of the age. This spirit was one of restless and
irreverent, though often very well-meaning, questioning of
all sorts of established beliefs and institutions. The ' Philosophers,' as the prevailing school of men in letters in France
were rather loosely called, were not content or disposed to take
anything on trust. In physics and metaphysics they attacked
the accepted principles of Descartes with the aid of the
English ideas of Locke and Newton. In politics they
affected admiration of the English system of representative
government and of limited monarchy. In ecclesiastical
matters they assailed the enormous wealth and political pre-
ponderance of the Church of Rome in France, while many of
them went further and questioned the truths of Christianity,
not a few advancing to the utmost length and ridiculing all
belief in the supernatural as superstitious. In history they
attempted for the first time to trace out general laws and
to systematise investigation. In natural science they were
untiringly, if perhaps not always very wisely, inquisitive. It
is rather curious that in pure literature this innovating spirit
should have given place to the profoundest distrust of innovation, and to the most implicit belief in the sanctity of
constituted authorities. The very men who most admired
the English constitution and the ideas of Newton and Locke,
for the most part regarded Milton as a tiresome preacher
and Shakespeare as a sometimes inspired lunatic. Dis-
trusting artificial forms of government and traditional beliefs
in religion, they accepted unquestioningly the most arbitrary
and artificial forms of poetry and the drama that have ever
prevailed. Even in prose fiction comparatively little advance
was made, and it was left to England to lead the way in this
respect also. Hence the fictitious literature of the period in

prose and verse is perhaps the least important of all its contributions to literary history, if we except the short prose tales which French for five centuries had rarely lacked. The strength of French eighteenth-century literature does not therefore lie in those branches where the form is of most importance, but in those where the matter is chiefly considered. Indeed almost every kind of composition was made to subserve the general purpose of attacking or at least questioning existing institutions. Five great names emerge. in the course of the century, those of Montesquieu, Voltaire, Rousseau, Diderot, and Buffon. These we shall treat in the order named, with the lesser writers who are more or less to be grouped with each. But first it is necessary to give an account of those older authors, who fill the space between the age of Louis XIV and the age of the Encyclopædia as it is sometimes termed. In the same way, after passing in review the five names just mentioned, we must notice such isolated authors as fall out of these groups. To observe the distinction of subjects in this period is, in a brief review, hardly possible, inasmuch as very many of the writers to be treated attempted many different classes of composition, and Voltaire, the chief of them, attempted nearly every class

The chief writer of the transition period in merit is undoubtedly Le Sage (1668–1747), the author of the famous novels *Le Diable Boiteux* and *Gil Blas*, and of a play, less read in England, but of great merit, *Turcaret*, besides a large number of other works. Le Sage, who presents some remarkable analogies to our own Fielding, had little in common with his contemporaries in his own country except wit and polish of style. It is significant that his two chief prose works both have their scenes laid out of France, and he is distinguished rather for his knowledge of human nature at large than for his special sympathy with the peculiarities of Frenchmen.

It is to this no doubt that his wide popularity in foreign countries is due. *Gil Blas* in particular has an almost Shakespearian quality of universal application, while at the same time the local colour, as it is called, of Spanish manners is strictly observed. Next in importance to Le Sage, but of a widely different character and a less original genius, was Fontenelle (1657–1757), the nephew of Corneille, a man of great acuteness and literary faculty, who, after attempting more independent kinds of work without much success, became a famous populariser of scientific and philosophical theories, and an almost unmatched composer of the half critical, half rhetorical treatises which the institution of the Academy made popular and profitable in France. His chief work is *Entretiens sur la Pluralité des Mondes.* Two poets of an artificial kind but not destitute of talent, Chaulieu (1639–1720) and La Fare (1644–1712), also belong to this period, and so in part does J. B. Rousseau (1670–1741), to be carefully distinguished from the more famous J. J. Rousseau. J. B. Rousseau was the best writer of the artificial lyric poetry which was alone possible on the principles of Boileau. His best work is of two curiously different kinds, one consisting of sacred odes and *Cantates* taken from Biblical sources, the other of epigrams of great wit and point. La Motte (1672–1731) was a writer of somewhat the same class as Fontenelle, but whereas the latter had entirely failed in tragedy, La Motte produced, in *Inès de Castro*, a play which had a great deal of success. He was, like all his contemporaries, a much better prose writer than poet, though few of his works in prose are of a kind to tempt the modern reader, consisting as they do chiefly of academical essays, controversies, and paradoxes, of the same kind as Fontenelle's. The comic series of Molière and Regnard was continued, with not more than proportionate falling off, by Destouches

(1680–1754) (*Le Glorieux, Le Philosophe Marié*), and a single tragedian, Crébillon (1674–1763), succeeded, by taking up the tradition of Corneille rather than of Racine, in producing work (especially in his *Rhadamiste*) of real dramatic and poetical value. Racine's son Louis (1692–1763) was a poet after a fashion, who studied Milton and wrote religious verse; and the Chancellor d'Aguesseau (1668–1751) revived, after a long period of eclipse, the reputation of French lawyers for cultivated eloquence. Nor perhaps should it be forgotten that Saint-Simon in point of time, though not of style and subject, rather belongs to this age than to the foregoing.

The first writer of great eminence belonging properly to the eighteenth century was Charles de Sécondat, better known by his title of Baron de Montesquieu (1689–1755), a gentleman of good birth in Guienne, and belonging to one of those families who were called in France *noblesse de robe*, from their continual and hereditary connection with the parliaments or provincial courts of law. Montesquieu was a great thinker and a great writer. His *Lettres Persanes* follow a favourite practice of the century, in satirising European manners and institutions by the mouth of an Eastern traveller, and in this, as in some minor works, he allows himself a certain amount of complaisance to the fashions and tastes of the time. His fame however rests upon his graver works, the *Grandeur et Décadence des Romains* and the *Esprit des Lois*, especially the latter. The 'Spirit of Laws' is one of the first books of any modern language which deal with history and politics on a wide system of philosophical enquiry. It is sometimes a little rhetorical in style, and very often its generalisations are a great deal too wide, but it is on the whole a very remarkable work, still calculated to stimulate the mind, especially in youth, to the taking of large and

comprehensive views. Moreover it is delightful from its
literary merit and its independence of thought, even when
the insecure basis of some of its speculations is fully acknowledged and understood. Round Montesquieu may be grouped
several lesser men who also attempted philosophical estimates
of politics and history, but without the careful study as well
as without the genius of the author of the *Esprit des Lois*.
That work is, among its many remarkable characteristics,
especially remarkable for the absence of the ignorant contempt for the political institutions of the middle ages which
was fashionable, as a consequence, in part, of the equally
ignorant contempt inculcated by Boileau for their literature.
In historical matters the chief representative of this contempt
was the Abbé de Mably (1709-1785), a writer of some merit,
but who did a great deal of harm by his indiscriminate
laudations of Greek and Roman institutions and manners.
Mably was perhaps more responsible than any other single
person for the nonsense talked in the days of the Revolution
at popular clubs and assemblies about Brutus and Harmodius
and Leonidas, and other misused heroes of antiquity. His
Entretiens de Phocion is his principal work. A much greater
man than Mably, and also a much more profound thinker,
was Turgot (1727-1781), who perhaps came nearer than
Montesquieu to the full philosophical conception of history
and historical development. His style is not remarkable, but
his matter is. Turgot conducts us at the extremity of the
century to Condorcet (1743-1794), his chief disciple, an
eloquent writer, but much less original than his master.
Turgot's works were principally short essays or discourses;
Condorcet's chief production is his *Esquisse des Progrès de
l'Esprit Humain*. Voltaire (between whom and Montesquieu
there was not a little jealousy) had less originality and range
of thought than his rival, but a much more miscellaneous

equipment of literary attainments. He wrote almost every-thing, long and short poems, plays, novels, imaginary con-versations, literary criticism, histories of greater or less length; and last, but not least, a desultory composition called a 'Philosophical Dictionary,' having some resemblance to Bayle's, but more definitely intended to stimulate religious doubt and disbelief. Voltaire was not an ardent reformer in politics, though—and this is the best point in his personal character—he was a most ardent defender of individuals who suffered from social and political abuses. His great literary weapon was ridicule, and this he could apply in almost every form and to almost every kind of subject. In purely serious work he was decidedly less successful. He began, as perhaps most writers of great talent have begun, with poetry, but, unlike the majority, he continued to practise it, and in many different kinds. Master as he was of ridicule, he seldom tried comedy, and his comedies are not good. But his first tragedy *Édipe*, was extremely and not undeservedly successful, and the best of his subsequent performances in the same kind (*Zaire, Alzire, Mahomet*) rank among the very best tragedies of the artificial kind. His so-called epic, the *Henriade*, is a very dreary poem; but he was a master of the lighter poetic forms, and in short satires, verse epistles, and the like, has but few superiors. *Le pauvre Diable* and *Le Mondain*, satires ranging over a wide social and literary field, may be especially men-tioned. It is however as a prose writer, not as a poet, that Voltaire best deserves his fame, and his performances in prose are even more miscellaneous than his performances in poetry. In absolute literary merit nothing probably that he has done exceeds his short romances, or rather tales, the best-known of which, and the best where all are good, are *Candide* and *Zadig*. For polished wit, knowledge of human nature, and adroit literary composition, these are masterpieces. His short histories (*Charles XII, Peter the Great*) are also excellent of their kind, and his longer works of a historical or semi-historical kind (*Siècle de Louis XIV, Essai sur les Mœurs*) are not inferior. There is however no possibility of here going through half of Voltaire's titles to literary distinction. Although given to violent resentment against those who attacked him, he was very well disposed towards literary beginners who looked to him for patronage, and in almost all of his lines of work he had followers and disciples. The most remarkable of these perhaps were Florian (1755-1794) and Marmontel (1728-1799), both of whom wrote light prose and verse of very various kinds. Marmontel's best-known works are *Belisaire* and *Les Incas*; Florian's, *Numa Pompilius* and *Gonsalve de Cordoue*, besides fables and suchlike trifles. The titles of these works indicate a favourite habit of the time, which was partly due to the example and popularity of *Télémaque*. This habit consisted of writing what we should now call historical novels with a purpose, the purpose being more or less definitely to inculcate the moral and philosophical ideas of the day. Under this head, though not quite in the same class, may be mentioned the Abbe Barthélemy (1716-1795), whose *Voyages du jeune Anacharsis* once had a considerable vogue.

A third great single name, and that of a man who had perhaps more practical influence than any one else in the latter part of the century, and on subsequent literature, is that of Jean Jacques Rousseau (1713-1778). An unhappy man, of melancholy temperament and weak will, Rousseau was the undoubted literary originator of what has since been known as sentimentalism. He found everything to be, as it seemed to him, wrong in society, and he set himself to preach that all should be altered. Men were to return to nature, political society was to be directly based on a social contract, education was to teach not accomplishments or learning but useful arts, the affections and emotions were to be given the, fullest play. These principles Rousseau enunciated and illustrated in a series of works very different from one another in form. Sometimes they were novels (*Julie*, *Émile*), and the first of these enjoyed such a popularity as probably no novel had ever enjoyed before. Sometimes they were regular philosophical discourses (*Le Contrat social*), sometimes meditations or essays or autobiography (*Lettres de la Montagne, Promenades d'un Solitaire, Les Confessions*). The language, if not as academically correct as was usual at the time, was singularly flexible and affecting, full of elaborate description of nature and of analysis of the strangest, and sometimes the meanest, parts of human character. On literature, on politics, on private manners and morals, Rousseau exercised a vast and almost unequalled influence.

As a preacher of the love of nature, and a describer of natural beauty, his mission was taken up by Bernardin de St. Pierre (1737–1814), who, with considerably less literary faculty, and infinitely less power and originality of mind, had the advantage of a wider experience and a less unhappy temperament. Like many of the authors already mentioned, Bernardin de St. Pierre has enjoyed the advantage of being very widely read, at least in his masterpiece. *Paul et Virginie* ranks with *Télémaque* as a book of general reading.

When Voltaire and Rousseau are mentioned, another name is frequently associated with them—the name of Denis Diderot (1713–1784). The importance of this writer is manifold, but lies perhaps chiefly in the realm of literary criticism. Voltaire was almost entirely conservative in this respect, and Rousseau cared less for the forms of literature than for the moral and sentimental ideas which it could be made to express. But Diderot, though himself a careless and very unequal writer, was an excellent and a most original critic, and he did perhaps more than any one else to lay the critical and formal foundations of the new school of literature which arose after his death, and in Germany even before it. His works are very voluminous, almost as much so as Voltaire's, and though inferior in elegance and perfection of workmanship to these latter, are far fuller of really original thought. They consist of plays (*Le Fils Naturel*), of essays on all sorts of subjects, chiefly philosophical, of art criticisms on the exhibitions of the Paris salon which are among the earliest and best examples of this class of literature, of novels (*La Religieuse*), and of a great many pieces almost impossible to class, the chief of which, and of all Diderot's works, is a singular character-sketch called *Le Neveu de Rameau.* But the bulkiest and perhaps the most influential of Diderot's literary undertakings was the famous *Encyclopédie*, in which he, with the assistance of almost all the greatest writers of France, undertook at once to give the world information upon all arts and sciences, and (indirectly) to attack what seemed to reformers the drawbacks of the existing system of church and state in France. His chief coadjutor in this undertaking was D'Alembert (1717–1783), a great mathematician and an accomplished writer; but, as we have said, almost all French men of letters, except the few who were on the orthodox and conservative side, and some even of these, assisted.

The names of these and other distinguished writers of a more or less practical or philosophical kind are so numerous that it is only possible to give them a brief mention. Condillac (1714–1780), the chief French metaphysician of the time, was a follower of Locke, who carried that philosopher's principles still further, and wrote in a clear and luminous manner. Helvétius (1715–1771) was a lively essayist who expounded what is called the selfish system of morals, in a book entitled *De l'Esprit*, and couched in the form of a regular philosophical treatise, though possessing little of the gravity usually expected in such work. Three abbés, Raynal (1711–1796), Galiani (1728–1787), and Morellet, wrote, the first on history, the second on political economy, and the third on miscellaneous subjects. Almost all the philosophical writing of this time is of the kind called materialist. A distinguished writer of this class, not yet mentioned, but earlier than most of those who have been mentioned, was La Mettrie (1709–1751), in whom many of the worser features of the time were illustrated, but who occasionally thought with much originality, and wrote (*L'Homme Machine*) with vividness and force.

The last of the five names set apart for special mention is that of George Louis Leclerc, Comte de Buffon (1707–1788), and like the others he may be set at the head of a class. Great part of the enquiring energy of the time was given to physical science, and Buffon was among the first who set the example of treating such subjects with attention to literary form. His style is pompous and rhetorical, wanting in directness and precision, and especially in what is called the *mot propre*, that is to say, simple graphic phrase without roundabout amplifications. But at its best, it is very eloquent and sonorous, partaking rather of the qualities of oratory than of written work. Buffon is still recognised as the chief master in French of this elaborate and artificial style. His *Histoire Naturelle*, a great work, in which he was assisted by humbler men, is his main production. Among other writers on physical subjects may be noticed here Maupertuis (1690–1759), and La Condamine (1701–1774), both of them geographical explorers as well as scientific students. The former, though not a despicable writer, is chiefly famous in literature for having been the butt of Voltaire's satire. The latter wrote an interesting account of his travels in South America.

Of names that do not readily fall under any of the groups yet mentioned, the following are the most important. In poetry the period was occupied, leaving Voltaire and his direct followers out of the question, by two pretty numerously attended schools, and by one or two single figures. One of the schools was that of writers of trifling *vers de société* mostly in a very artificial style, but often possessing considerable literary merit. Such writers were Bernis (1715–1794), Gentil Bernard (1710–1775), Boufflers (1737–1815), and Dorat (1734–1780). To these 'glow-worms of Parnassus,' as they were called, may be opposed another school of Anacreontic poets and epigrammatists who wrote songs, chiefly in praise of love and wine, light operas, etc. The chief of all these was Piron (1689–1773), a writer of great talent who very seldom made a good use of it. Collé (1709–1783) and Panard (1694–1765) also deserve mention. Malfilâtre (1733–1767) was a lyric poet of some merit, and Gilbert (1751–1780), who also died young, and perhaps in poverty, displayed not a little satiric faculty. Gresset (1709–1777), the author of *Ver-vert*, was however the chief minor poet of the time, and his masterpiece, the burlesque history of a parrot, is excellent. In drama, besides the names of La Chaussée (1692–1754), the inventor of what was called *comédie larmoyante*, or sentimental comedy, Marivaux (1688–1763), the novelist (*Les Fausses Confiances*), and especially Sedaine (1717–1779) (*Le Philosophe sans le Savoir*), must be mentioned. Gresset also wrote an excellent comedy (*Le Méchant*), and Piron one hardly inferior (*La Métromanie*). Among fiction writers the first place goes to the

Abbé Prévost (1697–1763), who among much unequal work produced a masterpiece of truth and pathos in *Manon Lescaut*, an immense advance on Madame de la Fayette's books, and hardly to be distinguished from the best modern novels. Marivaux's *Marianne* is good, and many writers of the time contributed to fictitious literature short tales after the fashion of Voltaire. An independent and striking moralist of the first half of the century was Vauvenargues (1715–1747), a man of rank, but not of fortune, who served in the army and died young, leaving a collection of maxims of great literary and philosophical merit. Thomas (1732–1795) was a writer of the academic discourses already noticed, and his works have ceased to be read, though they have merit as examples of the somewhat declamatory eloquence popular at the time. The Abbé Guénée (1717–1803), in his *Lettres de Quelques Juifs*, attacked the inaccuracies and blunders in which Voltaire too often indulged, with great wit and ability, and was indeed the chief worthy defender that orthodoxy had. Another great enemy of Voltaire was the critic Fréron (1718–1776), an acute though ill-tempered writer, to whom after a long period something like justice has been recently done. The presidents, Henault (1685–1770), and De Brosses (1706–1777) chiefly busied themselves with classical antiquity, the subjects connected with which both treated with considerable literary skill. Letter and memoir writing were still pursued, though on the whole with diminished success. The best memoirs of the century are probably those of Madame de Staal-Delaunay (1693–1750), the best letters beyond all comparison those of Mademoiselle de Lespinasse (1732–1776), a great friend of D'Alembert's. These latter are of an impassioned character, and of their kind are not to be surpassed in any literature. Among historians of different kinds, Rollin (1661–1741) may be mentioned as an example of careful labour, and Rulhière (1735–1791) of literary skill. The latter produced, in *Les Revolutions de Russie*, a short historical work of great elegance, and in his book on the dismemberment of Poland one of greater importance, but which unfortunately was not finally completed by the author. Rulhière, it should be said, was also a minor poet of considerable merits, though like many of his contemporaries he did not make the most amiable use of his talent.

Such is the summary, brief and necessarily imperfect, of the literature of this remarkable period of history. With the exception of the *Esprit des Lois*, it comprises no work which . unites literary merit, importance of scale, and practical value of contents in an extraordinarily high degree, but the number and multiplicity of its remarkable names and its remarkable books is very considerable. This number, as well as their comparative want of literary importance, at once necessitates and excuses a briefer review than has hitherto been given.

CHAPTER VIII.

FROM THE REVOLUTION TO THE RESTORATION.

FRENCH literature from the Revolution to the Restoration, or, to adopt more precise and accurate literary dates, from the death of Voltaire to the appearance of Lamartine, divides itself conveniently enough into two periods, the first of which contains a number of remarkable names, but none of the first rank; the second four or five of the first importance, but very few others to whom even the third or fourth can be assigned. The first period extends in point of time to the quenching of the most sanguinary civil dissensions at the incoming of the Directory; the second continues thenceforward. To the first class belong the names of Beaumarchais, Chamfort, Rivarol, Delille, Roucher, Volney, La Harpe and Chénier; to the second those of Chateaubriand and De Stael, with, at the extreme end of it and by a certain license, Béranger, Joubert, and Courier. It is remarkable that, with the doubtful exceptions of Chénier and Beaumarchais, no one of the first set (who may be generally described as a younger generation of *philosophes*) produced work which has continued to be highly valued, though all of them well deserve a place in literary history, as writers, and in some cases thinkers, of power. Their defect was that, with the single exception of Chénier, they merely followed up the tracks of others. Beaumarchais (1732-1799) was in some

sense an inheritor of Voltaire in his talent for the attacking
of social abuses with light and lively satire. But Beaumarchais' struggles with the légal iniquities of the *Ancien Régime*
were purely selfish, and thus ill replaced Voltaire's defences
of Calas and Servan and Lally. *Le Mariage de Figaro*, which
is Beaumarchais' strongest title to fame, is a clever satirical
drama of society, and has had its truth to nature testified to
by a popularity, in one form or another, of nearly a century;
but its attractions are not by any means purely literary.
Chamfort (1747–1794) and Rivarol (1753–1801) represented
another side of Voltaire's talent. They excelled especially in
what may be called drawing-room wit, scandalous stories,
epigrams, and detached aphorisms having reference to the
gossip of the moment and the political accidents of the
hour. Chamfort inclined to the Republican side, Rivarol to
the Royalist. Both attempted literary criticism, Rivarol not
without a good deal of success, while Chamfort wrote plays
which are deservedly forgotten. Their real titles to remem-
brance are those of anecdote-mongers and epigrammatists.
Rivarol in the latter capacity, and Chamfort in the former,
need fear hardly any competition. A contemporary and
rival of theirs in the formal essays on literary and other subjects which at this time engrossed a large share of the attention of literary men, was La Harpe (1739–1803), a disciple
of the *philosophes* who outlived most of his contemporaries,
and held for a time something like the position which Malherbe had occupied at the beginning and Boileau at the end
of the seventeenth century. La Harpe's principles of criticism
were not altogether different from those of these masters of
classicism, and his work has therefore lost much of its value,
though the writer was very far from being destitute of talent.
The poets of the time constituted what is known as the
descriptive school, which was strongly influenced by English

poetry.   The chief of them, Delille (1738–1813), was a man
of considerable literary powers, who simply devoted himself
to description, in verse of the artificial kind then alone
favoured, of everything in nature and art that could possibly
be described.   Delille's style was much better suited for
translation than for original composition, and his version
of the *Georgics* has considerable merit.   Earlier than Delille,
however, the example of this poetry had been set by Saint-
Lambert (1707–1783), an industrious contributor to the
Encyclopédie and in other ways a man of mark.   He imitated
Thomson's *Seasons*, in a poem of the same name, with great
applause.   The best of the poets of this school, though at
no time the most popular, were probably Roucher (1745–
1794) and Le Mierre (1733–1793), the former of whom in
Les Mois, and the latter in *Les Fastes*, displayed not a little
poetical fancy.   This fancy was unfortunately employed for
the most part in unpromising directions.   A poet of great
reputation at this time was Lebrun (1729–1807), who took
up rather the tradition of J. B. Rousseau than of any other
singer, and imitated his model both in elaborate odes of a
so-called lyrical kind, and in epigrams.   Lebrun, whom the
ignorance and pseudo-classical fancies of the time absurdly
united to call ' Pindar,' was a man of real, though as in the
case of nearly all his fellows, of misdirected talent.   A
better, though a still more unequal poet, was Parny (1753–
1814), whose early elegiac work attracted and deserved the
notice of Voltaire.   Parny, like many other French men of
letters of distinction, was a native of the colonies, and his
first work has a freshness of character as well as a grace of
form which contrasts very pleasantly with the hackneyed
mannerisms of his contemporaries.   Unluckily, as he became
older he became a much feebler writer, and fell into some of
the worst fashions of the time.   Similar to his early elegies

was the work of his friend and fellow Creole, Bertin (1752–1790).

Among these mediocrities or wasted talents, the figure of André Chénier (1762–1794) stands out very remarkably. With modern Greek blood in his veins, and himself a diligent student of the ancient tongue, Chénier sought to transfuse the spirit of that language into French verse, but neglected to fashion a new vocabulary and new metres for his purpose. Hence his work is of a singular character, the ideas and spirit being wholly different from those of his contemporaries, though the form is, outwardly at least, not to any remarkable extent dissimilar. His brother, M. J. Chénier (1764–1811), was a writer of talent in verse and prose, but far inferior to André, who perished by the guillotine in the last days of the Terror. M. J. Chénier lived to write dramatic works of doubtful merit, to take an active part in journalism, and to help, at least as a master of literary study, in the revival of old French literature. The weakest branch of French poetry at this time, though it was the most popular, was the drama. It has already been pointed out that the great drawback of the standard French tragedy was the confined character of its scheme, and the absence of any opportunity for the display of complicated incident or character. When, as was now the case, it had been constantly practised by five or six generations of writers, the limited number of scenes and situations that admitted of treatment according to its rules was completely exhausted. The differences of the new plays as compared with the old became a matter of the names of the characters mainly, and an intolerable sameness and staleness was the inevitable result. To make the matter worse, the artificial system in dramatic writing was extended to epic poetry, in which the French had never since the middle ages been skilful or fortunate.

The epic as well as the dramatic poets of the Republic and
the Empire were extremely numerous, but for the most part
of no literary value. It was in vain that Napoleon, who
would have liked his reign to be illustrated like that of Louis
XIV by literary as well as military triumphs, extended
patronage, or tried to do so, to literary men. Masterpieces
were not to be had for the asking. Here and there indeed
there appeared during his time of power writers of great
eminence, but they were either hostile to him or stood aloof
from him—with one single exception, who had hardly begun
to make his mark when the Empire came to an end. Yet
these persons are of great importance in French literature,
and deserve somewhat particular notice. Joubert, Chateaubriand, Madame de Staël, Paul Louis Courier, Béranger,
Joseph de Maistre, Bonald, are distinguished not merely
by great talent if not genius, but (with the exception of
Joubert and Béranger, who formed no new schools but were
rather the last and most brilliant disciples of older ones) by
the immense influence which they exercised on the literature.
and thought which came after them.

Joubert (1754–1824), was the last great pensée-writer of
France, and perhaps another cannot be expected until
thought and speech have gone through some considerable
changes. He differed from his predecessors, Pascal, La
Rochefoucauld and Vauvenargues, by including a much
greater variety of subjects in his short maxims. The whole
of a life which, though Joubert suffered from continuous
ill-health, was not a short one, was devoted to their
composition, and they were not published until after his
death. He has very well described his own method by
speaking of himself as tormented by the ambition of 'putting
a book into a page, a page into a phrase, and a phrase
into a word.' Like La Rochefoucauld, and perhaps unlike

any other writer of pensées, he has perfectly succeeded in his
attempt, achieving the utmost brevity without any corre-.
sponding sacrifice of fulness or clearness of meaning. His
observations on literary subjects are perhaps the best of all
his work, and it is remarkable that at the time at which
they must have been composed, literary criticism, and the
theory of poetical cómposition especially, was at the lowest
ebb in France. In politics, upon which he seems to have
thought much and strongly, he was a decided Conservative,
and might almost have been called a Reactionary. He had
early in life imbibed a distaste for the principles of the
philosophes, and the horrors and disturbances of the Revolution were not calculated to reassure a man of his temperament. On religion too his thoughts are noteworthy. Least
successful are those on the lower and more practical side of
morality, which perhaps requires for successful handling a
more active commerce with the world than Joubert enjoyed.

The Vicomte de Chateaubriand (1768–1848) was a
younger son of one of the noblest Breton families, many of
whose members suffered in the Revolution. He himself,
however, had already left the country before the actual
disturbances broke out, and spent a considerable time in
America, where he travelled much in the wilder parts of the
country, afterwards sojourning for a time in England, and
returning to France under Napoleon's amnesty. His early
hardships assisted his temperament—which was a curious
mixture of sentimental selfishness, poetical gloom, and
morbid vanity—to produce the peculiar colour of his work,
which may be described as that of a Christian Rousseau.
On the one side he delighted in depicting the manners of
savage tribes and the scenery of their countries (*Atala*, *René*,
Les Natchez, etc.), on the other he distinguished himself as
the rehabilitator of Christian ideas in religion, and monar-

chical ideas in politics. His adoption of these poetical and religious views was much more of a matter of sentiment than of reason. His learning was small and his powers of argument very weak. But he appreciated, and eloquently urged upon his contemporaries, the poetical and romantic side both of Christianity and of the old monarchical and aristocratic constitution. Soon his eastern voyages enabled him to unite his two lines of thought, and urge his favourite motives both by historical sketches and by landscape pictures. He was not an amiable man, and much of his writings rings very false to the ear, but he had real genius of an uncommon kind, and he was undoubtedly one of the chief propagators of the romantic movement both indirectly and directly in France as well as abroad.

Madame de Stael (1766–1817) was a daughter of the celebrated financier Necker. With Chateaubriand she occupies the foremost place in French literature between the Revolution and the Restoration. By birth and early connections she was inclined rather to the Liberal than to the Conservative side, but she had the strongest family reasons for disliking the extreme party of innovation in France, and she was bitterly opposed to Napoleon's tyranny, an opposition which subjected her to not a little inconvenience. Her best-known works are some early treatises of a half literary, half philosophical kind; two novels, *Corinne* and *Delphine*, the first of which had a great share in directing French enthusiasm towards Italy and Rome ; and a book on Germany, which in the same way directed the French to the literature and thought of their formerly patronised and despised neighbours. In all these works a certain superficiality of thought strikes the reader now, as well as the absence of grace in the style, and the presence of trite and commonplace expression. But they were extremely stimulating to

the readers of their own time, and were of especial service
because they suggested to Frenchmen that their own intellectual position was not so absolutely superior to that of
all other nations as they had been accustomed to think.
The strong reaction which the anti-religious and anti-
monarchical excesses of the revolution provoked, was represented in the less ornamental departments of literature by
two remarkable writers, De Maistre (1754–1821), and De
Bonald (1753–1840). These partisans of the elder order of
things did not, like Chateaubriand, confine themselves to a
kind of sentimental regret for its associations and accom-
paniments; nor did they, like the Liberal school, blame the
Revolution for the practical tyranny which it had substituted
for the nominally despotic but really indulgent government of
the eighteenth century in France. On the contrary they
were absolutists of the severest type, though they reached
their conclusions by different roads. Both uphold what is
called theocracy, but with Bonald the immediate delegate
of God is the King, with De Maistre it is the Pope. Both
wrote with great energy, and frequently in a very effective
style, but Joseph de Maistre is, in originality of thought and
literary merit, far the superior of the two.

Béranger and Courier date in point of literary celebrity
considerably later than the writers just mentioned, but as
they lie quite outside the Romantic movement proper, and in
Béranger's case can hardly be said to have exercised the
least influence upon it, they are best mentioned here. Paul
Louis Courier (1773–1825) served as an officer in the army
during several campaigns, and until he was past middle life
attempted no literary work, except translations from the
classics, especially Greek, and study of the French writers of
the seventeenth century. Both these studies inspired him
with not a little contempt of the eighteenth-century writers,

who had, as he saw, fallen as far away from the classics of
France as from the classics of Greece and Rome. It was
only after the Restoration that these elaborate studies in
language bore fruit in original work. Courier did not in the
least share the aristocratic and monarchical and ecclesiastical
reaction, and was in this respect a thorough political child
of the eighteenth century which in literature he despised.
He therefore heartily threw himself into the pamphlet war
which the advanced Liberal opposition kept up against the
Government. In point of form and style these pamphlets
are among the most admirable things in literature. They
most nearly resemble Swift's *Drapier's Letters* in their elaborate simplicity and the fine irony which abounds in them,
but they are written with almost more delicate art.

Pierre Jean de Béranger (1780–1857), again, is almost
wholly of the past, even more so than Joubert; for while the
ideas of the latter are mainly those of the nineteenth century,
Béranger is only the chief and concluding member of the
school of French song-writers which extends over the whole
of the eighteenth. These songsters sang of love and wine, of
politics and social follies, and Béranger did the same, but
with a more earnest purpose, a greater metrical faculty, and
a wider range of subject. He was an ardent devotee of the
Napoleonic legend, as it is called; that is to say, the theory
which represents Napoleon as the greatest and most glorious
chief of the French nation. This, however, is most appa-
rent in him after the overthrow of the Empire, it being the
general habit of the song-writer to be in opposition. Béranger was sincerely attached to his country, though his
attachment often took the form of not very intelligent abuse
of other countries, and his common sense, good nature, and
desire to promote the welfare of France and Frenchmen as
he understood it deserve acknowledgment. It may be noted

that he had learnt something from his immediate predecessor Desaugiers (1772–1827), a fluent and musical singer, who however kept to the older style of song, and is much less remarkable for earnestness and purity of purpose than Béranger himself. But for this very reason he is sometimes preferred to Béranger (unjustly it must be confessed) by those who differ from the younger singer on political points, or who think that a song-writer ought not to touch serious subjects at all.

A few other writers deserve mention. Sénancour (1770–1846) was a meditative writer of some originality and more suggestiveness, belonging to the school of dissatisfied sentimentalists. Benjamin Constant (1767–1830), a famous parliamentary orator and politician, belongs to literature as well as to politics, and wrote novels and philosophical treatises as well as numerous pamphlets on the Liberal side. This side was also espoused by a considerable number of philosopher-statesmen whose principal aim was not, as that of the *philosophes* of the eighteenth century proper had been, to destroy, but rather to build up. The chief of these was Royer Collard (1763–1846). This philosophical school, resting chiefly on the Scottish school of metaphysics, produced not a few writers of merit. In a very different order of literature, Xavier de Maistre (1763–1852), the younger brother of Joseph, wrote his charming *Voyage autour de ma Chambre*, a model of discursive writing which has been frequently imitated since. The same writer, in *Le Lépreux de la Cité d'Aoste*, attempted the narrative more definitely, and may be joined to a small band of novelists of the time of the Empire, of whom Fiévée (1767–1839) is perhaps the chief, and who anticipated in some degree the immense development which prose fiction was shortly to receive. H. Beyle (1783–1842), who wrote under the name of Stendhal, began the novel of psychological analysis. His work (*La Chartreuse de Parme, De l'Amour*) had great influence both on his younger contemporaries and on later writers, and is very remarkable both in style and substance. The dramatists of the Empire, as of the Republic, were of so little value that in the present sketch it is unnecessary to burden the page with their names. But one of them, Nepomucène Lemercier (1771–1840), was also a poet, and in both capacities showed a considerable if unequal talent. Another poet of the time deserving a passing mention is Chénedollé (1769–1833), nor perhaps should Fontanes (1757–1821) and Arnault be left out. The former is chiefly of importance to the history of literature because he was under the Empire charged with the patronage of it by Napoleon, and did his best to encourage men of talent and faculty superior to his own. Arnault (1766–1834) was a graceful writer of fables. This style of composition has always enjoyed a considerable popularity in France, a popularity which may be presumed to be due in part to that of La Fontaine's masterpieces, and to the natural emulation and imitation which these have excited in succeeding writers of the last two centuries.

CHAPTER IX.

VERY soon after the completion of the great period of political upheaval and of foreign conquest which terminated at Waterloo, a revolution almost as great in degree came upon French literature. In the last four chapters we have surveyed the fortunes of that literature from the time when, at the beginning of the seventeenth century, it definitely severed itself at once from mediæval tradition and from the unfettered innovations and experiments of the Renaissance. We have seen it go through four phases of what is vaguely, but with sufficient expressiveness, called classicism. The first, the age of the origins of the classical tradition, is occupied for the most part in slowly excluding certain forms and manners as barbarous, and in regulating those which are allowed to remain by narrow and artificial rules. The second, the age of Louis XIV, exhibits the most brilliant results that can possibly be obtained from such a system of literary criticism. The polish, the proportion and the ordered beauty which come from a strict adherence to rules appear in full lustre, and as yet there is no sameness or monotony. In the third period, that of the eighteenth century, the decadence is obvious and rapid. Much good literature is written, but its goodness depends either on the interesting nature of the subject treated, or on the individual power and expertness of the writers, and as soon as this fails, literature, especially imaginative literature, sinks into a state of aridity and sterility. The fourth or revolutionary period manifests this decadence at its very worst in its ordinary literature, though all its writers of merit, save one or two, indicate more or less unconsciously means of recovery. The comparative quiet of the Restoration period, a quiet not of apathy or political deadness, but of fairly good social order, gave occasion for the new birth to take place, and this new birth was what is called the Romantic Movement.

To understand what this movement was and what it did, we must point out more precisely what were the faults of the older literature, and especially of the literature of the late eighteenth century. They were in the first place, an extremely impoverished vocabulary, no recourse being had to the older tongue for picturesque archaisms, and little welcome being given to new phrases, however appropriate and distinct. In the second place, the adoption, especially in poetry, of an exceedingly conventional method of speech, describing everything where possible by an elaborate periphrasis, and avoiding direct and simple terms. Thirdly, in all forms of literature, but especially in poetry and drama, the acceptance for almost every kind of work of cut and dried patterns, to which it was bound to conform. We have already pointed out that this had all but killed the tragic drama, and it was nearly as bad in the various accepted forms of poetry, such as fables, epistles, odes, etc. Each piece was expected to resemble something else, and originality was regarded as a mark of bad taste and insufficient culture. Fourthly, the submission to a very limited and very arbitrary system of versification, adapted only to the production of tragic Alexandrines, and limiting even that form of verse to one monotonous model.

Lastly, the limitation of the subject to be treated to a very few classes and kinds.   Now as a matter of formal criticism, no one had yet arisen to point out these evils and their remedies, though in some cases much that Diderot had said went directly to the root of the classical, that is, the Malherbe-Boileau tradition.   But for many years critics, even while omitting to discover, or at least to indicate, the cause, had ridiculed and condemned the result.   Rivarol and La Harpe, neither of them disinclined to classicism in the abstract, and the latter in his old days a fanatical defender of it, had waged war against the poetasters of their time.   The influence first of Rousseau, then of Bernardin de St. Pierre, then of Chateaubriand, had directed men's minds rather to the study of nature and of savage countries than to the acceptance of the conventional French-classical world of civilised convention. The last-named writer, acting together with the political reactionaries of his generation, and assisted by the studies of antiquarians, had· revived an admiration for the middle ages, which had for centuries been more neglected and despised in France than anywhere else.   Madame de Stael, by her novels and her book on Germany, had in a different order of thought helped to break down the idea that France was necessarily a model and pattern of the universe, and German literature had powerfully assisted the ferment.   Lastly, at the close of the period, and when peace had been restored, the works of Scott and of Byron exercised an immense influence, the former by turning attention to mediæval romance, the latter by suggesting, perhaps on some hints from Goethe and Chateaubriand, the modern romantic dissatisfaction and despair which have contributed so much good work and so much bad work to literature. Hence, by 1820 everything was favourable to a revolution in literary art.   Even Courier, the ardent opponent of royalist

religious and mediæval ideas, had, as has been said, a profound contempt for eighteenth-century style, and recom-
mended that nothing later than Louis XIV should be taken
as a standard.

The spirit of literary camaraderie has always been strong
in France, and it was assisted to produce an effect in this
instance by the new institution of journalism. More than
one periodical, especially *Le Globe*, bore a very great
share in bringing about the romantic movement. But before
noticing this it will be well to give some account of two
remarkable and distinguished writers who, falling out of the
list of romantics proper, stimulated the movement almost as
powerfully as any of its forerunners already mentioned, or
as the chief partakers in it themselves. These were Lamartine (1790–1869), and Lamennais (1782–1854). The former
derives directly from Chateaubriand, though he was in the
first place a poet, while Chateaubriand was essentially a
writer of poetical prose. Lamartine at a comparatively early
age began to write poems (*Méditations*, *Harmonies*, etc.),
presenting in outward form considerable resemblance with
the accepted lyric poetry of the later classical period, but
characterised by a much greater freshness and truth of poetical
expression and thought. The note of gentle and chastened
sentiment and of a kind of tearful sympathy with nature
dominates, and there is a remarkable absence of striking
expressions, of bold metrical experiments, and of the varied
and unrestrained choice of subjects which characterise the
romantics proper. But though the verse of Lamartine
expressed the new spirit in old forms, and in a hesitating
way, it still expressed it. Lamennais, on the other hand,
while also deriving in style not a little from Chateaubriand,
was exclusively a religious writer, even at a late period of his
life, when the disfavour of the Church of Rome drove him

into a kind of irreligious philosophising. His *Essai sur l'Indifférence en Matière de Religion* had a great effect, and established him as the future leader of the more ardent and . reforming ecclesiastical party. His style was vigorous and bold, not indeed at first so broken and mysterious as it afterwards became in his most famous book, the *Paroles d'un Croyant*, but very different from the chastened pattern of standard French prose. Two poets of some note, Alexandre Soumet (1780–1845) and Casimir Delavigne (1793–1843), also lie out of the list of romantics proper. The former was chiefly a dramatist, and in his *Fête de Neron* and other plays endeavoured to give life and movement to the drama without wholly breaking with the classical tradition. Casimir Delavigne also wrote plays, for the most part bad ones. In his *Messéniennes* he displayed considerable poetical faculty alloyed with much of the false rhetoric and declamation of the eighteenth century.

The romantic movement proper divides itself into two stages, the first of which passed before 1830, the latter subsequently to the Revolution which extinguished legitimate monarchy in France, while both, subsequently confounding themselves, extended till nearly the end of the reign of Louis Philippe in full militant .vigour, and have not lost their influence to the present day. The distinguishing names of the first are Victor Hugo, Sainte-Beuve, Alfred de Musset, Emile and Antony Deschamps, Prosper Mérimée, Charles Nodier, Alexandre Dumas, Alfred de Vigny; of the later, Théophile Gautier and Gérard de Nerval, with in each case, but especially in the latter, not a few minor names to supplement those of greater importance.

The immense literary work of Victor Hugo began within four years of the battle of Waterloo, by the establishment of the journal called, oddly enough, *Le Conservateur Littéraire*,

in which the poet, though then only a boy of seventeen, took
part with his brothers Abel and Eugène, and by degrees with
all the rising spirits of the new movement, as well as with
those of an elder generation, such as Chateaubriand. But
he soon appeared as an independent author, and his Royalist
Odes, his mediæval *Ballades*, his barbaresque *Orientales*, and
the somewhat more sober but not less beautiful volumes
which followed under the titles of *Les Feuilles d'Automne*,
Les Voix Intérieures, *Les Rayons et les Ombres*, etc., soon
placed him at the head of French poetry, a position which in
more than sixty years of life he did not lose. His innovations
in drama were not less than those which he affected in poetry
proper. *Cromwell* was not performed, but *Hernani* served
as the battlefield between classics and romantics, and resulted
in the decided victory of the latter. It was followed by many
other dramas which had an almost equal success. The main
characteristics of Victor Hugo's poetry are an extraordinary
boldness of thought and phraseology, a complete contempt
of artificial rules as to versification, diction, and choice of
subject, and above all the most surprising command of
musical language, and of a rushing style which carries away
the reader whether he will or no. The young writer soon
showed himself to be possessed of an equal faculty for prose
and for poetry. His earliest prose works were romances of
a wild character, drawing their scenes and characters from
uncivilised and barbarous times. *Han d'Islande*, an impossible romance of Norway, full of the most grotesque
extravagances, is nevertheless admirable in the vigour and
picturesqueness of not a few of its passages. *Bug Jargal*, in
which the scene is shifted to St. Domingo, is but little inferior,
while *Notre Dame de Paris*, in which the author shifts again
to mediæval times, at once took rank as the most striking
though one of the most unequal prose romances of the

century, during which, till his death in 1885, Victor Hugo
remained at the head of French literature, and perhaps of
the literature of Europe.

As Victor Hugo was the poet of the new movement, so
Sainte-Beuve (1804–1869) was its critic; and, like the poet,
the critic retained for the whole of his life the superiority
which he obtained at the beginning of his career. The first
work of importance which Sainte-Beuve composed was the
series of *Tableaux de la Littérature Française au XVIème
Siècle*, which he published in the *Globe*. This remarkable
work at once reinstated the older writers of France in the
place which since Malherbe had been denied them, and
directed the rising generation to the proper places to look
for models of language and style. For a time Sainte-Beuve
endeavoured by purely original work to obtain a place for
which he was not fitted, his poems and works of fiction
(*Volupté*, *Joseph Delorme*, etc.), being of no extraordinary merit.
But he soon recovered from this failure, and devoting himself
afresh to purely critical work, became perhaps the most
celebrated prose critic of any age, founding indeed an entirely new school of criticism, as Victor Hugo has founded
an entirely new school of poetry. The latter had said ' Never
mind the rules, is the poem good?' and the former set himself to work to criticise not merely poems, but all literature
on the same principle. For this purpose he took immense
pains to enquire exactly into all the influences which might
have acted upon his subjects, and endeavoured to represent
these to his readers in order that they might judge rather
what the author intended to do, than whether he had done it
according to some pre-established regulations for the guidance
of authors. In this his later career Sainte-Beuve was judged,
partly from personal motives, to have ceased to be a
Romantic, but this was simply because the true import of the

literary revolution was mistaken. He worked his work, Hugo his, and the effect of the lives of the two men has been an entire revolution of literary principles and practice in every country in Europe, except where, as in England, native genius had anticipated the necessity of any such change.

Under the banners of which in poetry and criticism these two men were the standard-bearers, many champions fought, some of whom only half agreed with the principles of the leaders, while others, from individuality and eccentricity of genius, parted early from the army. Charles Nodier (1783–1844), an older man than most of his friends, was a charming writer, but did not sufficiently devote his genius to the task of mastering one particular field. Yet his short tales rank among the best in French. Emile (1795–1871) and Antony Deschamps (1809–1869) did good service, not merely by original work, but by translating great foreign classics, such as Dante and Shakespeare. Alfred de Vigny (1799–1863), a writer of fastidious taste and of some indolence, chose his subjects on the new principles, but handled them with a precision and classical elegance rather suggestive of the old. Auguste Barbier wrote, as Delavigne had written before him, satires of a somewhat obsolete form but of admirable vigour and elegance. Alexandre Dumas (1803–1870), bringing to the service of romanticism an almost unmatched fecundity of imagination and readiness of pen, began by composing dramas of an extravagant but powerful cast, but soon subsided into the composition of historical romances, which are perhaps the very best of their kind, or which, if not the very best, share that position only with Scott's. Prosper Mérimée (1803–1870), a man of exact taste and great scholarship, began by forging imitations of Illyrian and other barbaric poetry, according to a general

fancy of the early Romantics.   He soon however quitted the
school as far as outward companionship went.   But he continued to write in a marvellous prose style, and to compose
short tales and novels of extraordinary merit in construction
and subtlety in depicting character.   Last, and perhaps, next
to Hugo, greatest of the earlier romantics, comes Alfred de
Musset (1810–1857), a lyric poet of incomparable grace,
though of a somewhat Byronic school, the author of exquisite
small dramatic pieces and of miscellaneous works of great
merit.   The exertions of these leaders, especially those of
Victor Hugo, were after 1830 supported by a band of younger
recruits, of whom the principal were Théophile Gautier and
Gérard de Nerval.   Théophile Gautier (1807–1872) became
the most perfect poet in respect of poetical form that France
has ever produced, while he was hardly less remarkable as a
writer of romances and short tales, as a critic of literature
and art, and as a describer of foreign countries.   In most of
these capacities Gérard Labrunie (1808–1855), who called
himself De Nerval, was but little if at all less distinguished.
It has been already observed that though almost all the
writers of this period exhibit the influence of the Romantic
school, many, even in the imaginative departments of literature, cannot be directly classed as belonging to that school,
while others, from the character of their work, employed as
they were upon serious or scientific subjects, had no cause
for expressing adhesion or aversion to the prevailing doctrines.   Yet among both these latter classes it is almost an
invariable rule that the principles of the Romantic school in
its saner and less extravagant forms are exemplified.   Foremost among the novelists of the time must be mentioned
Honoré de Balzac (1799–1850), the author of a wonderful
series of studies of French life, largely tinged by the author's
idiosyncrasy, and even by his imagination, but still faithful

in principle and in the main to the truth of nature. Next to Balzac comes Aurore Dudevant (1793–1876), universally known by the name of George Sand, one of the most voluminous of writers, and perhaps for that reason not likely long to retain the position which she has hitherto held. Her later studies of provincial life are admirable, more so than the powerfully coloured but too often extravagant and tedious novels written in her earlier days. Charles de Bernard (1805–1850) excelled in short sketches, for the most part of Parisian society, which he wrote with a pleasant mixture of satire and sympathy that in some sort inspired our own Thackeray. Jules Janin (1804–1874) began by some novels in the extremest romantic style, but ended as a theatrical critic, in which capacity he achieved great popularity and influence. Léon Gozlan was a writer of miscellaneous literature often remarkable for felicity of style and construction. So also Alphonse Karr, one of the few survivors of the 'generation of 1830,' has written on a vast variety of subjects, all of them of the kind, called light literature, which has of late years been popular in France as well as elsewhere. Madame Charles Reybaud, X.B. Saintine, Jules Sandeau, Frederic Soulié, Emile Souvestre, Eugène Sue, contributed work more or less remarkable to the immense total of fiction of literary merit which France has during this century produced.

Of dramatists, besides those already mentioned, Eugène Scribe (1791–1861), the most prolific of recent French dramatic authors, but distinguished from the romantic school by a loose and careless style and by vulgar and unpoetical thought, deserves the first place. Ernest Legouvé (b. 1807) is another popular dramatist of a semi-romantic kind, while the success of the *Lucrèce* of Ponsard (1814–1867) has been taken as the epoch at which the first flush of romanticism died out and a classical reaction set in. But there was no real reaction, and the literature of the last forty years has been, whether professedly or not, always under the influence of the movement at the head of which we have placed Victor Hugo and Sainte-Beuve. Among lesser poets, Jean Reboul (1796–1864), a southern poet of some elegance, F. Viennet (1777–1868), who clung to the old models, and chiefly wrote fables, Madame Tastu and Madame Desbordes-Valmore (1787–1859), the most successful of modern French poetesses, Hégésippe Moreau (1810–1838), a poet of some power, who died young, Victor de Laprade, who till his death the other day continued with grace and not without power the tradition of Lamartine, Auguste Brizeux (1806–1858), a Breton of talent, and J. Autran (1813–1877), who, like Laprade, represented rather Lamartine than Hugo, deserve attention.

Although Sainte-Beuve far excelled all the critics of the earlier part of the century in talent, there were many who must be ranked beside him, some of whom anticipated if they did not quite equal his reformation of the critical method. Of his seniors, J. J. Ampère (1800–1864), an amiable historian of Rome and of Roman French literature, Abel Villemain (1790–1870), who was among the first to give intelligent attention to foreign literatures, deserve notice; and among his contemporaries and juniors, Saint-Marc Girardin, Planche, Nisard, and others.

The destruction of the old régime and its salons has somewhat destroyed the reputation of French literature for memoirs, private letters and similar work, but it has on the other hand produced an abundant crop of regular histories. Barante (1782–1866) produced in a picturesque style many learned works on the older annals of France, among which his *Histoire des Ducs de Bourgogne* is the chief.

F. Guizot (1787–1874), also famous as a statesman, gained a considerable place in literature with various writings on French and English history; his rival, A. Thiers (1797–1877), began a long series of historical works by his History of the French Revolution; Henri Martin produced the most comprehensive and perhaps the most trustworthy of histories of France, and J. Michelet (1798–1873), in a series of works, partly purely historical, partly busied with political and social philosophy, developed one of the most original of French prose styles, a style which has sometimes been compared to that of Mr. Carlyle. With Michelet is generally mentioned Edgar Quinet (1803–1875), also master of a rather poetical style. They were both extreme Liberals; both were attracted, notwithstanding their Liberalism, to the study of the middle ages, and both were professors at the same time in Paris, where their lectures drew crowded audiences. On the opposite, or Catholic side, but still with a strong leaning to political Liberalism, may be noticed another brilliant lecturer and ardent student of the middle ages, Frédéric Ozanam (1813–1853), who died young.

In philosophy, the French Scottish metaphysical school of Royer Collard and his fellows was succeeded by what is called the eclectic school of Victor Cousin (1792–1867), an eloquent writer who endeavoured to execute a movement in philosophy somewhat parallel to the romantic movement in literature, by borrowing some of the theories and processes of the German thinkers. There was more rhetoric than thought in Cousin's system, and towards the end of his life he abandoned philosophical writing altogether and betook himself to literary essays on attractive characters in French history. His influence however was very considerable on the younger generation, and many writers were impelled by it to study the history of philosophy and to

compose works of more or less literary value on that
subject.

The prose works mentioned in this chapter show an
alteration in French prose style which is at least as important as that which the language of poetry underwent.
It has already been said that the results of the classical
traditions upon prose were much better than those upon
poetry. In accordance with them two things were considered incumbent upon a French prose writer, to treat his
subject in a regular and orderly manner and to be above
all things clear and precise in his ·expressions. Of these
conditions the prose of the eighteenth century frequently
complies with the first and always with the second. The
last writer on this classical model was Paul Louis Courier,
and on the whole prose has not been improved by the
romantic movement. The average French prose writer since
1830 has been less careful of his plan, less intent upon
making his meaning clear, than his predecessors. But on
the other hand the language has gained a great deal of
ornate and picturesque prose which was impossible with the
limited vocabulary and phrases of the elder style. The
manner of Michelet has been already mentioned, and it is
hardly to be surpassed for pictures of the bold and striking
order either in landscape or in historical event. So
that of Lamennais is admirable for solemn religious eloquence, while that of Edgar Quinet comes between the two,
and is weakened by a certain tendency to sentimentalism.
On the other hand, the short tales and descriptive literature
which occupied so many of the romantics proved very
favourable to prose of the extremely careful and exquisite
kind. Prosper Mérimée and Théophile Gautier carried the
powers of the language probably as far as they will go in
this way, Gautier inclining rather to a rich and highly

coloured style of diction, Mérimée to one simpler and some-what more of the classical in kind. Gautier's descriptions of foreign countries are hardly to be matched in any language for the vividness with which they bring the scenes described before the eyes of the reader.

CHAPTER X.

THE contemporary literature of France concerns us rather in so far as it is an outcome of the history and tendencies already sketched, than as it is composed of the performances of individual writers. Yet inasmuch as it is impossible to exhibit the former without giving some account of the latter, no great deviation from the method observed in former chapters will be necessary. The literature of the last thirty or forty years in France has been for the most part complexioned by the Romantic movement, of which an account was given in the last chapter. It is true that from time to time writers of more or less talent have arisen who have affected to question the necessity and value of that movement, and to deny the merit of its chief literary representatives. But when we turn to the actual work of these, as of other French men of letters, we find the practical triumph of the movement recognised in the most practical way. No one for half a century has with the least success attempted to revive the old dramatic theory of limited interest, of arbitrarily confined action, of confidants, of long rhetorical tirades, of artificial noble sentiment and more artificial interchange *de soupirs et de flammes*. No one in poetry proper has reverted to the standards of La Harpe, no one in fiction has attempted to take his characters from a conventional assortment of cut-and-dried personages. Even at the present moment the most obvious and most discreditable failures of French literature are due rather to an unintelligent exaggeration of Romantic principles than to an abjuration of them. The work which was done in 1830 was to all appearance done as finally as the work of all literary reactions is done. The absurdities which arise from perversion and travestie of their principles die out or are violently overthrown, what is weak in them asserts itself for a time, and is after a time exploded; but what is strong and good and true remains and is permanently incorporated in the structure and tendencies of the language and the literature. This is true, to confine ourselves to the present subject only, of every great change which has passed over the literature of France, whether the author—to speak more philosophically, the chief representative—of that change be Alain Chartier, or Clément Marot, or Pierre de Ronsard, or François de Malherbe, or Nicolas Despréaux, or Victor Hugo. Every one of these men has contributed, according to his lights and in the measure of his powers, something to the perfection of the language which all of them used and the literature which all of them loved and in different degrees honoured. No one of them has been absolutely right or wholly wrong, though the varying degrees of influence which they have exercised have enabled their followers to do less or more good work as the case may be. The innovators, the suggesters of foreign models, such as Chartier and Ronsard and Hugo, have perhaps done more good than the formalists and conservatives, such as Marot and Malherbe and Boileau, because there is an undoubted tendency in Frenchmen and in the French language to stereotype rules and habits, and to fall into a childish admiration of their own ways and a vain reproduction of those ways. But their

opponents have had this merit—that they have perhaps been
more thoroughly in accord with the genius of the nation, and
that they have therefore enabled the average writer of prose, if
not of verse, to do better work than has been done by such
average writers in the periods dominated by their rivals.
The unfavourable effect which, with some brilliant exceptions,
has been produced upon French prose by the exaggerations
of the Romantic movement has been noticed in the last
chapter, and is still more noticeable in the productions of
living men of letters in France.   Nor is it as yet at all obvious
what influence is likely to put a stop to the degeneration.   It
may perhaps be said to be due in part to the increase,
noticeable in French literature of this period, as indeed in
most of the other literatures of Europe, of periodicals and
newspapers.   In no country has the newspaper attained
greater power and popularity than in France, and in none
has it attracted so many of the best writers.   It is fair to
allow that, putting certain poetical works out of the question,
the best books of the last forty years in France are, for the
most part, volumes of reprinted essays, criticisms, and the like.
Though the general effect on style may have been bad, the
new system of criticism started and practised by Sainte-
Beuve transformed this department of literature, from one
of the most arid and unattractive of literary forms, into
one of the most fascinating.   Almost all French writers
since 1830 have given themselves up, either permanently or
for a time, to it, and also to the writing of fiction, for which,
owing to the *feuilleton* system, or practice of including an
instalment of fiction in almost all periodicals, daily and
weekly and monthly, there has been a very great demand.

   During all but the whole of this period, as of the last, M.
Victor Hugo continued to be the representative poet of France,
though after the termination of the period which we have

fixed as that of the Romantic movement proper he ceased to write dramas for the stage. The establishment of the Second Empire, to which he was violently opposed, turned his genius in the direction of satire (*Les Châtiments*) and of eloquent historical moralising on the fate and history of man (*La Légende des Siècles, Les Contemplations*), in which he persevered till his death in 1885. He produced with astonishing fecundity every few years volumes of generally admirable verse in different styles, the finest being, perhaps, *Les Quatre Vents de l'Esprit.* Meanwhile the first school of Romantic poets gave way to another, in which the influence of Théophile Gautier was more directly represented than that of Victor Hugo, though the latter was still regarded as the general master. Gautier had from the beginning been extraordinarily careful about the form of his work, and the peculiarity was imitated by the younger school, of whom the most remarkable were Théodore de Banville, Charles Baudelaire, and Leconte de Lisle. The first of these poets has spent much of his time in reviving and popularising the elegant artificial forms of verse which have been noticed as being chiefly cultivated in the fourteenth and fifteenth centuries. The last two relied chiefly upon the presentation of unusual scenes or sentiments to their readers. M. Leconte de Lisle in especial, a very learned poet, translated many classical authors, and went by turns for his inspiration to Greece, to Scandinavia, and to the East. Under the auspices of these writers there grew up in the later days of the Empire a school of poets who have gone under the name of *Parnassiens*, from the habit of publishing from time to time collected specimens of their work under the title of *Le Parnasse Contemporain.* They were very numerous, and for the most part attained great mastery over the technical part of their art, though there may be perhaps rather too little spontaneity about them. Some of these, as M. François Coppée and M. Sully Prudhomme, diverged after a time from the school in which they began, and adopted different methods: while the Parnassians proper have sometimes exaggerated the tendencies of the three masters mentioned above. Of the many writers of verse who have appeared during the last fifteen years, two only, M. Guy de Maupassant and M. Richepin, have shown really original talent, and in both cases this talent has been too often directed to unworthy objects.

After the termination of Victor Hugo's great series of romantic dramas no new work of the same kind was for some time attempted. The most popular dramatist of the early part of the Second Empire was Emile Augier, a skilful dramatist of the comedy of manners. Later, Augier's eminence was shared by Alexandre Dumas the younger, and by Victorien Sardou. The former has devoted himself rather to studies of morals, the latter to pictures of contemporary manners. M. Sardou has frequently attempted more serious pieces, without the success which has attended his lighter and more satirical efforts. The Empire was not favourable to a high class of theatrical literature. But since its downfall efforts have been made to revive the romantic drama in a form not quite so English or Spanish as that affected by the dramatists of 1830. M. Henri de Bornier's *Fille de Roland* and his *Noces d'Attila* are plays which set the example, followed by some success and imitation, of pieces different from the ignoble burlesques and spectacles which were long the fashion. One kind of dramatic composition, which was brought to perfection by Alfred · de Musset, remains to be noticed. This is the *Proverbe*, a short piece with few characters, in which some well-known maxim is illustrated. Musset's pieces of this kind are examples of very delicate and refined art, both as drama and as pure literature. He has not been fully equalled by any of his successors, though several of them, with M. Octave Feuillet at their head, have done good work in their attempts to tread in his steps. The purely literary merit of theatrical writing has however rapidly declined of late years, and its distinction even in the lighter forms has been made good chiefly by writers hardly belonging to the present generation. The poet Théodore de Banville has produced some excellent work, the best-known of which is *Gringoire*, a short romantic comedy on the satirist and farce-writer of the fifteenth century. M. Ludovic Halévy, now an Academician, obtained his reputation chiefly by librettos to the music of Offenbach. Of late, however, he has turned his attention to pure fiction; and has won, not only in the admirably Voltairian sketches of the *Famille Cardinal*, but in scrupulously virtuous stories, such as *L'Abbé Constantin*, a remarkable popularity. Probably the best playwright, in the proper sense, of the last thirty years has been Eugène Labiche (1815–1888), who struck with extraordinary success a vein between comedy and farce, his working of which, in at least *Le Voyage de M. Perrichon*, has almost, if not quite, succeeded in adding something permanent to literature. M. Edouard Pailleron, like MM. Halévy and Labiche an Academician, has also done work of much literary quality, among which, in different styles, *Le Monde où l'on s'ennuie* and *Le Chevalier Trumeau* deserve remark and reading.

The famous novelists of Louis Philippe's reign have been succeeded by a group hardly less remarkable, though perhaps inferior in individual talent. Two writers, MM. Erckmann and Chatrian, revived interest in the novel of stirring incident, which the popularity of the works of George Sand, Balzac, &c., had somewhat dimmed, by a series of tales of the revolutionary wars, distinguished by great freshness of manner, by much interest of narrative, and by a very healthy and pure

tone of morality. The elaborate analysis of motive and
character of which Balzac had set the example was carried
to a still further pitch by Gustave Flaubert (1821–1880), who
also enjoyed the advantage of greater power of the purely
literary kind, and of immense and careful study. Besides his
novels of analysis of modern character, Flaubert produced
some tales on ancient topics full of splendid colouring and
imaginative incident. M. Octave Feuillet, rather following
George Sand, has made himself the novelist of the higher
fashionable life in France. Ernest Feydeau worked a somewhat similar vein, but with less refinement and more doubtful
morality. M. Cherbuliez (like many other distinguished
French writers, a Genevese by birth) has written a large
number of novels usually displaying great literary skill, and
generally of good moral tone. M. Droz has added to the
list volumes of short stories, showing much wit and accurate
observation. A little earlier came a writer of genius who
lived unhappily and died young. This was Henry Murger
(1822–1861), the special novelist of what is called 'Bohemian'
life, that is to say, the life of the young artists, musicians, and
literary men who have always haunted Paris in great numbers.
Murger had great truth to nature and a command both of
pathos and comic power. Edmond About (1828–1885), a
most lively narrator and possessed of some of the qualities
of Voltaire without his range, never did anything quite so good
as might have been expected from him : but, like many men
of letters in the present day, he spent much of his talent in
journalism. During the last decade or a little more a school
of so called 'Naturalist' writers has grown up whose avowed
purpose is to consider, in subject and treatment, not artistic,
still less moral qualities, but only a certain faithfulness to
what is or is assumed to be fact. This school, which, without
much justice, traces itself to Stendhal, Balzac, and Flaubert as

originals, shows some signs of declining; but two of the strongest, if not the best, of recent French novelists, M. Zola and M. Alphonse Daudet, belong to it, as well as, in his prose work, M. Guy de Maupassant. Unfortunately, in all the work of this school, and especially in that of M. Zola, contempt of decency is pushed to an extreme as inartistic as immoral. Two other writers deserve to be mentioned— M. Ohnet for his extraordinary popularity with readers, which is only equalled by the disfavour with which his work is regarded by all competent critics, and M. Viard ('Pierre Loti') who has embodied his foreign experiences as a naval officer in a style of much elegance and some affectation.

Of the various critics whom the general adoption of Sainte-Beuve's method has called, as already mentioned, into notice, three are perhaps deserving of special mention. M. Taine, whose History of English literature has made him better known in England than most French writers, has carried his master's practice rather than his theory to the utmost possible limits,—limits which indeed often produce an absurd result, as is amply to be seen in the book just mentioned. M. Taine's theory, broadly stated, is that every author is a 'product of his circumstances' rather than an individual genius, so that by examining those circumstances he can be fully explained and understood. This theory he has exemplified with much ingenuity and skill, but too frequently with the result of mis- understanding, and therefore misleading. A more sober critic is M. Edmond Scherer, whose only defect may be said to be a too great tendency to judge authors by the standard of his own agreement or disagreement with their principles and choice of subjects. A third critic, now dead, who resembled rather Gautier than Sainte-Beuve in his careful choice of language and the pictorial character of his work, was Paul de St. Victor (1828–1881), whose critical acuteness was not always equal to his literary faculty. A collection of his earlier critical essays, entitled *Hommes et Dieux*, contains, with much unequal appreciation, some of the most admirable writing of the kind anywhere to be found; and had he completed and revised the series of studies on the Drama of the world, on which he was latterly engaged, it might have been, if it is not still, the most remarkable specimen of a certain kind of nineteenth-century style and critical method in France. This is entitled *Les deux Masques*, and in the vivid pictorial manner, not seldom overwrought, in which it endeavours to exhibit the stage of Greece, it is thoroughly characteristic. In years immediately recent there has been more appearance of the devotion of talent to criticism than in most other literary departments, and M. Paul Bourget, M. Jules Lemaître, and others have attracted much attention. It is perhaps also worth noticing, that translations of a high order of literary merit have been commoner in French of late years than in most other tongues. François Victor Hugo's *Shakespeare*, and M. Leconte de Lisle's versions of many of the Greek poets, are among the most remarkable instances.

In what have usually been considered the more serious branches of literature few finished works of the highest merit have been produced during the last thirty or forty years, and those mostly by writers who have been mentioned in the preceding chapter. The principal, if not the solitary exception, is M. Ernest Renan, who in his position as an ecclesiastical historian and critic has emitted many disputable opinions, but has clothed them in language of great elegance and individuality, which is likely to give him a lasting place in the history of French literature. The direction of M. Renan's studies has been, as has been said, chiefly ecclesiastical, but the manner of them is much the same as that of a large number of scholars, less distinguished as literary artists, who

have devoted themselves to criticism and research in philosophy, theology, history, political and literary, philology,
and other branches of modern science. Thus in France, as
in other countries, men have rather been engaged in collect-
ing materials for future literature, than in manufacturing it
themselves. Of these various branches of enquiry, too
numerous to be dwelt on here, the study of Old French
language and literature may be singled out both as characteristic and interesting in itself, and as specially suitable to our
present purpose. It has been said that at the close of the
last century some attention was paid to the long neglected
writers of old France by the critics of the Empire. The be-
ginnings of the Romantic movement stimulated this yet more.
An eloquent exponent of the study was found in Fauriel
(1772–1844), and soon the patient industry of Germany began
to found a regular science of Old French, and to draw forth its
treasures from the obscurity of manuscript. French scholars
themselves were not behindhand: with M. Paulin Paris at
their head, they set to work to disinter the buried literature
of the twelfth, the thirteenth, the fourteenth, and the fifteenth
centuries, while the professed littérateurs of the romantic
school, headed by Sainte-Beuve and Théophile Gautier,
performed the same service for the printed but almost equally
forgotten books of the sixteenth and early seventeenth. A
great venture of the studious Benedictines, the *Histoire
Littéraire de la France*, was received and continued, and for
the last sixty years not a year has passed without the publi-
cation of editions of the poems, chronicles, romances, and
plays of the past. The immense riches of early French
literature have as yet prevented the task from being completed, but by this time a sufficiently full acquaintance with
at least the main features of every part of French literature is
possible to the student. Perhaps the best idea that can be

given of the gain resulting from these studies may be suggested
by mentioning that the first three chapters of this primer, the
materials of which are now open to any one, could not have
been written sixty or seventy years ago without a life's
labour, and that the very names of most of the boo s and
authors mentioned in them were then unknown, even to the
best-informed Frenchmen.   The Chansons de Gestes were
known only in late prose versions, the Fabliaux only by
extracts and analyses, the Arthurian romances, like the Chansons, only in late prose forms, and the lyric poems, the
mysteries, and the less noteworthy prose works, not at all.
Boileau, in the seventeenth century, had made French literature
practically begin with Villon, and though there had always been
isolated students of the middle ages, they had been exceptions,
and had laboured under great difficulties.   One of the most
illustrious workers in the field of French literature of all times
was the late M. Littré (1801–1881), author of the only complete and satisfactory French dictionary.   M. Littré was an
ardent student of the middle ages, contributed to the *Histoire
Littéraire*, and in many ways earned the gratitude of his
fellow-students.   But even his work does not include anything like an exhaustive lexicon of the older language, and
indeed, as will be evident from what has just been said, such
a lexicon was until recently hardly possible.   It has, however,
now been begun, and it is probable that if M. Godefroy, who
has undertaken it, is able to finish his work, a few years will
see the completion of the apparatus necessary for the study
of French literature.   At present an exaggerated idea prevails
even in France of the difficulties of the language, and the
French are as a rule less well acquainted with their own
early writers than any other nation which has reached an
equal point of civilisation.   Perhaps however, though there
is more excuse for us, England is not quite in a position

to throw stones at •them for their shortcomings in this respect.

Such is a brief view of the present state of French literature, and such, as far as this little book can attempt to show it, have been the fortunes of this great section of human thought and human art as applied to written speech. It is perhaps more interesting than any other literature, because of the long space of time which it covers without any sensible break in the manifestation of real and living literary activity. In all other literary histories, ancient and modern, there is to be met with either a short period of consummate activity, or a long history broken by gaps of trance and suspended vitality. The literatures of Greece and Rome are examples of the first; all modern European literatures, including our own, of the second. The oldest monuments of English literature are older by perhaps six or seven hundred years than the oldest monuments of French literature proper. But they are not intelligible to modern Englishmen without much pains, and they are followed by centuries of sterility and stagnation. The history of French literature from the *Chanson de Roland* to the latest work of M. Victor Hugo is continuous without a single break; and the *Chanson de Roland* itself can, as has been said, be read by a person only acquainted with modern French with at least as much facility as that with which a modern Englishman can read Chaucer. Thus we have spread over a period of nearly eight hundred years, a complete picture of the thought, the character, and the history of the nation. Nowhere can the student find such an opportunity of determining how far the literary utterances of a people correspond to their national character, what tendencies in the long run assert themselves most in literary forms, how far foreign influence can decide the intellectual and artistic development of peoples, how far consummate individual genius can produce perfect work against what may be called the national grain. The answers to these questions can only be obscurely indicated in a small hand-book like the present, and the student must seek his full satisfaction in larger works, or in his own independent reading. These pages have chiefly endeavoured to set before the learner such a general view of the outline of French literary history as he may best be able to fill up for himself afterwards. No writer of great importance has been omitted, and the literary tendency of all such persons has been indicated, though of necessity in a kind of shorthand. It has been found, in the course of many generations of scholars, that such a general view is of no small value in order to prevent the student in his reading from attaching undue value to isolated authors who happen to attract him, and from passing over others who deserve careful and elaborate attention. The filling up of a correctly drawn outline is comparatively easy, while study without such an outline must, in the circumstances of most students, too often result in misapplication and mistake.

INDEX.

THE END.

www.ingramcontent.com/pod-product-compliance
Lightning Source LLC
Chambersburg PA
CBHW030904050726
47500CB00009B/1020